MOURNE
SEAFOOD BAR

The Cookbook

MOURNE SEAFOOD BAR

THE COOKBOOK

ANDY REA
BOB MCCOUBREY

Mourne Seafood Bar
34–36 Bank Street
Belfast, BT1 1HL, Northern Ireland
www.mourneseafood.com

ISBN 978-1-9097511-0-1

Graphic design:
Dean Pauley
www.deanpauley.co.uk

Photography:
David Pauley – The Studio
(Dust jacket and recipe photography)
www.thestudio-photography.com
Nigel Jamison
(Landscape photography)
www.nigeljamisonphotography.com
Khara Pringle
(p.10, p.14, p.193)
www.kharapringlephotographic.com
Northern Ireland Tourist Board
(p.17)

Printing:
Nicholson & Bass

CONTENTS

FOREWORD

I've known Andy Rea for about 20 years and when I first met him I recognised a spark in him that I knew would drive him on to become the accomplished chef and teacher he is today.

He always possessed a passion for cooking, learning and innovating new ways of doing things. We worked together for about a decade and I sincerely hope he learned some of that from me!

Andy also loves his home city of Belfast and has been a consistent champion for local produce and so this book is a coming together of all the things that make up his vibrant character.

One of his great qualities is that he makes cooking look easy. That's because of the decades of hard work he has put in learning his craft and also because he has natural good taste, judgement and skill.

His relaxed and easy-going nature makes him an excellent teacher because he genuinely wants anyone with an interest to gain the skills required to produce amazing dishes in their own home.

He wants to share his skills and expertise and demystify the art of great cooking and he wants people to feel like good cooks by giving them the skills and techniques that are achievable.

Andy's philosophy has always been get it right but keep it simple and in Mourne Seafood Bar you will experience this as well as wonderful fresh fish dishes served with passion and love.

That attractive and approachable way of doing things also radiates from the pages of this book as he presents dishes that are full of flair, flavour and zest while at the same time easy to replicate without intimidating even the novice in the kitchen.

That is actually quite a difficult thing to pull off and reflects Andy's enthusiasm and quiet confidence in what he does so well.

There are no short cuts to becoming a great chef but in this book Andy has shared the distilled knowledge of his years of experience to ensure that you can make dishes to enjoy and be proud of.

I truly believe that to be a great chef you need to be a great teacher because to teach you must first fully understand the principals and skills of what you are doing.

I always really enjoyed working with Andy Rea and believe his food has been a huge influence on the many local chefs and restaurants that now make Belfast the celebrated 'food' city it is today.

I am confident you will also get the same pleasure from cooking and eating the dishes that Andy has shared in this book. He has provided you with a lifetime's experience to give you the confidence to explore the wonderful world of seafood with passion and flair.

Andy Rea fully deserves all the success and plaudits he attracts and I wish him the very best on his culinary journey.

Paul Rankin

INTRODUCTION

'To eat seafood is to hear the gulls, feel the sand and
taste the sea!' – *Mourne Seafood Bar*

Welcome to the world of great seafood! Think of this book
like an oyster – a little bit of patience and knowledge will let
you open a world of hidden seafood delights. I'm thrilled to be
able to share with you a lifetime of knowledge and passion for
the culinary wonders of the sea. And I hope that you will gain
the knowledge necessary to cook and enjoy delicious seafood
meals for any occasion.

Great food is best enjoyed shared and that is why I wanted
to give both loyal customers of the Mourne Seafood Bar and
new converts alike the skills to recreate a little bit of our magic
in their own kitchens. The recipes in this book are tried and
tested favourites served daily in our restaurants.

Not a day goes by without customers asking me and my
chefs questions about how we sourced or cooked a particular
fish or what ingredients we used in our dips and dressings.

We love to share so very often we scribble down a recipe
on the back of an order docket and give it to our curious
customers to take away and try at home. Of course doing it this
way meant some of the subtleties of preparation and the all
important 'here's what it is supposed to look like' photo are
missing. So writing this book means I can share those recipes,
tips and skills comprehensively with more people in the hope
it will help spread my passion for this style of cuisine.

So why seafood and why Mourne Seafood Bar in the middle
of Belfast? For me, it has been a long journey that started when

I met my business partner Bob McCoubrey about eight years ago. Along with his wife Joanne, he was running Mourne Seafood nestled at the foot of the Mourne Mountains in Dundrum.

Dundrum is a coastal village so locating Mourne Seafood there made sense because customers could be served fresh seafood straight from the little family-run fishing boats moored in nearby Portavogie and Kilkeel or from the shellfish beds in Carlingford Lough.

Bob himself was part-time oyster farmer and he and his wife Joanne had a real passion for good quality fresh seafood prepared simply. Their motivation for opening the original Mourne Seafood was to fulfil a personal longing to be able to eat good quality seafood prepared well and at a reasonable price because that experience was not available anywhere else in Northern Ireland at that time.

Having spent time in Martha's Vineyard, I already knew the glories of seafood but I had all but given up trying to get the Irish to try the treasure trove of ingredients to be harvested from the seas around our island nation.

The infrastructure for the delivery of seafood in Northern Ireland just didn't exist and the demand from consumers was also lacking. Excuse the mixed metaphor but it was a 'chicken and egg' scenario – the market wasn't there because people didn't want fish and people didn't want fish because the market for it didn't exist. So fish on the menu could be a hard sell as diners tended to stick with what they knew. Sadly, seafood was relegated to something only the most adventurous palate would tackle.

Mourne Seafood in Dundrum was a revelation to me and it helped rekindle my passion and determination to put fish

back centre stage where it belongs. So impressed was I with Bob's restaurant venture and the gusto by which his loyal local customers consumed his fresh seafood, that I wanted to share that glorious experience with as many discerning customers as possible.

And so our partnership was born. Bob had the expert knowledge of sourcing local seafood and I had the experience to make a great restaurant work. Our common goal was to migrate the inspiring menu based on fresh seafood and the relaxed atmosphere of Mourne Seafood in Dundrum and take it to a wider audience by opening a second location in Belfast.

But how do you translate the experience of a laid-back coastal bistro restaurant into the middle of bustling Belfast? Or perhaps the question should be why put that experience in our capital city? It's easy to forget that Belfast is actually a port. Architecturally, Belfast has developed in a way that means it has effectively turned its back on views of the water, with our port hidden from public view and reduced to being simply functional.

The port of Belfast is now a place where the cargoes of the world are loaded and unloaded and most peoples' experience of it is a place to catch the ferry rather than catch a fish!

But seafood once played an important role for the residents of this city as it provided a cheap source of nutrition to even the poorest of Belfast's inhabitants.

Evidence of the key role oysters once played in Belfast coincidently turned up right on the doorstep of Mourne Seafood Bar during the renovation stage when we discovered quite a number of oyster shells in the foundations of the building. These discarded shells were thought to date from the 19th century when oysters were the equivalent of modern day fast food and consumed in great numbers by the poor as a cheap and nutritious snack.

Oysters and herrings were sold at that time by Irish-speaking street vendors called Fadgies who resettled in Belfast from their native Omeath after the Famine.

It's therefore perhaps fitting that my restaurant is located in an area that has a long history of the consumption of seafood. It feels like things have come full circle.

In the intervening centuries, we fell out of love with our culinary maritime heritage. Seafood had attained a reputation of being exotic – dangerous even – and for many people it was something they were required to eat only on Fridays as part of their religious observance. Not a good combination when it comes to the enjoyment of food.

On top of that, what fish was caught off our coast was generally shipped abroad because better prices could be commanded on the international market.

For decades, just jars of vinegary cockles and mussels, cod for battering or a bit of limp brown fish to be boiled in milk were really all that was available in our local shops.

There were very few dedicated local seafood sellers and most were viewed by consumers with suspicion – except by the rare pioneering foodies who were 'in the know'. So inevitably, fish and seafood just didn't excite anyone's palate and few people had the skills or knowledge to prepare it. This meant it was ignored or even vilified by many.

But then came the era of cheap flights and that meant more and more people were travelling abroad and enjoying the seafood dishes so commonplace in many other parts of the world. This exposure to the delights of fish in foreign climes rekindled in people a love of seafood.

Langoustines, mussels, scallops, monkfish, prawns, squid and octopus became little taste postcard memories of holidays in the sun and people wanted to relive that joyous experience when they got home. So the time was right to offer them a place in the city that not only fulfilled their desires to eat good seafood, but also reflected the relaxed laid-back dining style enjoyed by our European neighbours.

In 2006, the building that is now home to Mourne Seafood Bar came on the market and since no other restaurant in Belfast was serving the quality of fish and seafood that we thought people wanted, we took the risk to make Bob and I's dream a reality. And it was a risk. The location we chose, whilst a few hundred yards from the city's main shopping street, still hadn't been gentrified and we didn't even know for sure if there was an appetite for this style of cuisine in the city.

Even the building itself, a derelict bar, needed a lot of renovation on a shoestring budget. But I instinctively knew the quality of food and wonderful atmosphere I could offer would draw even the most culinary unadventurous in.

Having trained with Belfast's foremost culinary innovator Paul Rankin and been a chef in some fantastic restaurants during my career, I knew I had the skills, knowledge and passion to give Belfast the dedicated seafood restaurant it deserved.

I wanted to create a destination restaurant stripped of pretention where diners could come in and get a great lunch for under a tenner, enjoy a relaxed atmosphere and experience the actual theatre of seafood. I wanted it to be a place where locals would bring their overseas visitors to showcase the best fresh ingredients Northern Ireland has to offer.

I wanted to offer delicious, innovative and honest food that has been locally sourced at a price that is accessible to most.

In short – it was my mission to democratise seafood and allow people to fall in love again with our fantastic food heritage enjoyed in a relaxed contemporary setting.

Mourne Seafood Bar is the realisation of that dream and its ongoing success vindicates my theory that the people of Northern Ireland want to eat great seafood.

I still get a tingle of excitement when I see the regular queue forming outside Mourne Seafood Bar just before lunchtime as people wait to buy fresh, seasonal produce from our wet fish and seafood counter located at the front of the restaurant.

This reflects a growing confidence on the part of consumers to buy, take home, cook and enjoy freshly prepared seafood as part of their normal daily diet.

The pace of our evolution of food in Northern Ireland in the last 30 years has been unbelievable and I would now class Belfast as one of the top five food destinations in the whole of the UK and Ireland.

I believe that food culture reflects the character of the place where it is enjoyed. Locally, we have a tremendous history of good, honest, traditional home cooking and subsequently we have high culinary standards.

We are also curious about food and open to learning more and the quality and culinary diversity of restaurants in Belfast and beyond reflects our inquisitive interest in food.

Now people want to incorporate fish more and more into their daily diet as a healthy, tasty and nutritious alternative to meat.

This book will equip you with the skills to create family favourites, delicious and exciting meals to impress your dinner guests and recipes of simplistic beauty that can quickly and easily be conjured up after a hard day's work.

But to achieve your full potential you will need fresh, seasonal ingredients – the majority of which should be locally sourced if possible.

This is the foundation to Mourne Seafood Bar's success and it will also be the key to your success when cooking at home.

I still source my fresh fish daily from local fishermen and the seasonal variations they present means my menu must be dynamic and flexible enough to utilise whatever they net.

It's worth the effort though. Because we're a small island our local boats don't go out for a long periods of time, just one or two days at the maximum, so the fish is always fresh and that makes all the difference.

For me, the star of any of my dishes is the main ingredient – fresh fish and seafood. The less you do to it, the better it is. So in Mourne Seafood Bar I serve fish with heads and tails still on, mussels in pots and crab claws in their shells.

Part of the enjoyment of seafood is the effort you have to put in to get at the best bits. Prying open crab claws, shucking oysters, winkling mussels out of their shells or picking succulent fish from its bones satisfies a primeval urge in us all. It's both base and sophisticated. Rustic, yet urbane. But most of all it's delicious!

So set aside any preconceptions that you might have that fish is difficult to cook as we are going to keep it simple but skilful.

Drop the fussy rules associated with table manners, because, trust me, your fingers are the best tools for getting to the tastiest bits of seafood. It is time to expand your knowledge of the wide range of seasonably available fish caught in our local waters and get swept away on a wave of enthusiasm for all things fishy.

I want to inspire you to cook and eat seafood with enjoyment and a sense of confidence.

And through the pages of this book I will share with you my pearls of wisdom and knowledge as you embark on your culinary voyage. And remember – the world is your oyster so get shucking!

Andy Rea
Head Chef of Mourne Seafood Bar, Belfast

TECHNIQUES

In an ideal world you would buy your fish either whole or on the bone whenever possible. Not only is it easier to tell this way how fresh the fish is, but any trimmings can be used for stock.

But in reality the scaling, the gutting, the boning, all the messy jobs are done by your fishmonger. Most fishmongers will do it for you at no extra charge. So you don't have to worry about anything but the cooking.

Along with Belfast Cookery School we have put together a few easy to follow videos. The symbol on your recipe will direct you to the appropriate video. These can be accessed by scanning the 'QR' code or visiting the web address.

HOW MUCH TO BUY
· Whole fish 1 kg (about 2 lb) Serves 2
· Whole fish, gutted, with head and tail removed 450–500g (about 1 lb) Serves 2
· Steaks or cutlets 500g (1 lb) Serves 2–3
· Skinned fillets 500g (1 lb) Serves 3–4

GUIDE TO QUALITY
Fresh whole fish have bright, full eyes and gills that are pink-red and have a pleasant sea smell. The flesh is elastic, springing back when gently pressed.

HOW LONG TO KEEP
Fresh fish should be used as soon as possible after purchase. It will keep in the refrigerator for 2–3 days. Keep fish on a plate covered with waxed paper, foil or plastic in the coldest part of the refrigerator.

TECHNIQUE	SYMBOL	QR CODE
Preparing mussels youtu.be/N-bLzA0zilg		
Preparing lobster youtu.be/byv9hqgUEIY		
Preparing flat fish on the bone youtu.be/9wxOFzFFtiY		
Preparing flat fish fillets youtu.be/QBd2VYXZ7NA		
Preparing oysters youtu.be/b29imVQn6II		
Preparing round fish youtu.be/v-BRZKvU4Yc		
Preparing round fish fillets youtu.be/mg6TLznXg_g		
Preparing John Dory youtu.be/mg6TLznXg_g		

APPETISERS

· 1 packet rice paper
· 400g cooked prawns or shrimp
· 50g cooked beansprouts
· 75g cucumber, cut into fine strips (no seeds)
· 50g carrot, grated
· 25g scallions, chopped
· 25g coriander, chopped
· 25g mint, chopped

Vietnamese dipping sauce:
· 2 long red chillis, chopped (no seeds)
· 1 clove garlic, minced
· 1 tbsp. grated palm sugar or light brown sugar
· 2 tbsp. lime juice
· 3 tbsp. fish sauce
· 2 tbsp. rice vinegar

Alternative fish:
cooked lobster or crab
Preparation time: 20 mins

PRAWN SUMMER ROLLS WITH VIETNAMESE DIPPING SAUCE

1. In a large bowl mix together the prawns, herbs and vegetables. Season with sea salt and a pinch of chilli pepper. **2.** Carefully remove 8 sheets of rice paper and make sure none of the sheets are broken. Brush each sheet with cold water and lay down on your worktop. Leave for 1 minute until rice paper is soft enough to roll. **3.** Divide prawn salad between the 8 rice papers in a long narrow strip and roll tight into a cigar shape. Cut each summer roll into 3 or serve whole. **4.** Once made, they need to be served immediately and eaten.

VIETNAMESE DIPPING SAUCE

1. Pound the chillies and garlic into a fine paste with a pestle and mortar. **2.** Add sugar mix and the rest of the ingredients plus 2 tablespoons of water. **3.** Store refrigerated in an air tight container. Keeps for 2 days.

'Summer rolls can seem bland on their own, but dipping each bite into the sauce adds a different dimension.'

Serves 4

- 800g fresh langoustines, split in half lengthways
- ½ bottle chipotle tabasco
- 200g soft butter, salted
- 1 tbsp. chopped parsley
- ½ lemon, grated zest
- 4 cloves garlic, minced
- pinch of smoked paprika

Preparation time: 20 mins
Cooking time: 10 mins

GRILLED LANGOUSTINES WITH SMOKED CHILLI BUTTER

1. Pre-heat oven to 225°C. **2.** Mix tabasco, butter, parsley, garlic, zest and paprika. **3.** Lay langoustines flat on baking sheet, cut-side up. **4.** Using a brush or palette knife, spread chilli butter over langoustines, bake for 8 minutes. **5.** Serve straight from the oven with lemon. Serve with crusty bread.

'The chipotle sauce is what gives these langoustines their irresistible little kick. Chipotle is a tabasco-style sauce made from smoke-dried chillies that originate in Mexico so it has a little South American sass. Combined with the spiciness of the paprika, the depth of flavour of the garlic and the silkiness of the butter, this dish is a symphony of flavour. Forget knives and forks and dive in with your fingers, as they are the best tools for eating langoustine. Don't panic if you can't get fresh, live langoustines as this dish still works well with cooked ones – just half the cooking time. Which means half the time to wait for this feast!'

Serves 4
- 1 packet Chinese dumpling wrappers (available in any Asian supermarket)
- 150g white fish (cod, whiting, hake etc. no skin or bones)
- 50g shellfish (scallop meat, prawn meat, crab etc. diced)
- 4 scallions, finely chopped
- 1 clove garlic, minced
- 1 tsp. fresh minced ginger
- 25g chopped coriander
- a good pinch of chilli powder
- 1 egg

Tomato and cardamom ketchup:
- 1 tin (or 400g) of cherry tomatoes or plum tomatoes
- 1 medium onion, diced
- 1 black cardamom
- 1 tbsp. ginger, minced
- 4 cloves garlic, minced
- 6 green cardamom, toasted and crushed
- 1 tsp. chilli powder
- 1 tsp. paprika
- 1 tsp. garam masala
- 1 ½ tbsp. tomato purée
- 125g light brown sugar or palm sugar
- 75g cider vinegar
- fish sauce, to season

Preparation time: 15 mins
Cooking time: 10 mins

SEAFOOD DUMPLINGS WITH TOMATO AND CARDAMOM KETCHUP

1. Over a medium heat, place a large pot of water, season and bring to a soft boil. **2.** In a food processor, add white fish and ½ egg, season with sea salt and chilli powder. Process until smooth then add scallions, coriander, ginger, garlic and shellfish. **3.** Season gently and use the pulse setting on your food processor, just enough to mix but not enough to fully process and set aside. **4.** Lay dumpling wrappers one by one on a worktop, 16 in total (unused wrappers can be frozen for later use). Spoon a 'marble' sized ball into the centre of each wrapper, brush the edge of the wrapper with the remaining egg and fold and seal to form a half circle, squeeze together the 2 sides to seal, repeat until all are filled and sealed. **5.** In batches, place dumplings in boiling water for 4–5 minutes. Remove with a perforated spoon and allow to cool naturally. **6.** Dumplings can be made ahead, to finish, shallow fry or deep fry until golden. **7.** Serve with napa slaw (see page 183) and tomato and cardamom ketchup.

TOMATO AND CARDAMOM KETCHUP

1. In a saucepan over a medium heat, add a drizzle of oil and the onion, season and cook until golden. **2.** Then add ginger, garlic and spices and cook out for 2 minutes. **3.** Add tomato purée, cook out for 3–5 minutes, and then add the rest of the ingredients. **4.** Cook out over a low heat for 30 minutes. **5.** Purée in a blender and season with fish sauce to taste.

SMOKED MACKEREL PÂTÉ

Serves 4
· 100g smoked mackerel fillets, no skin
· 75g cream cheese
· ½ tsp. Worcestershire sauce
· juice of 1 lemon
· a few dashes of tabasco
· sea salt and cracked black pepper
· 1 tbsp. chopped chives

Preparation time: 10 mins

1. In a blender, process everything except for the chives. Once processed, fold in the chives, taste and adjust seasoning.

SMOKED SALMON PÂTÉ

Serves 4
· 100g smoked salmon
· 100g cream cheese
· juice of 1 lemon
· 1 tsp. wasabi powder
· 1 tbsp. chopped dill
· 1 tbsp. minced shallot (rinse chopped shallot in cold water before adding salt and pepper)

Preparation time: 10 mins

1. In a blender, process everything except for dill and shallots. Once processed, fold in the dill and shallots.

'Both pâtés work well on crostinis, wheaten and malt bread.'

Serves 4
- 6 oysters, shucked
- 30g cucumber, grated
  (no seeds)
- 20g pickled ginger, shredded
- 2 tbsp. of Kikkoman soy
  'reduced' salt variety
- 1 tbsp. lemon juice
- ½ tsp. powdered wasabi

Preparation time: 15 mins

Serves 4
- 6 oysters, shucked
- ¼ Granny Smith apple, peeled
  and cut into 2mm dice
- 2 tbsp. cider vinegar
- 1 small shallot, peeled and
  finely diced

Preparation time: 15 mins

Serves 4
- 24 shucked oysters

Thai dressing:
- 30g grated palm sugar
- 30g cucumber, finely diced
- 1 tsp. pickled ginger,
  finely diced
- 1 red chilli, finely diced
  (no seeds)
- zest of ½ lime
- juice of 1 lime
- 1 tbsp. fish sauce
- 1 tbsp. chopped coriander
- 1 tbsp. vegetable oil

Preparation time: 15 mins

OYSTERS JAPANESE STYLE

1. Mix together soy, lemon juice and wasabi powder in a small bowl and set aside. **2.** Divide evenly on each oyster, cucumber and pickled ginger, then spoon soy dressing over cucumber and oysters and serve immediately.

OYSTER WITH APPLE MIGNONETTE

1. Mix all of the ingredients and spoon dressing over each oyster just before serving.

OYSTERS WITH THAI DRESSING

1. Mix all of the ingredients together. **2.** To serve, spoon dressing over freshly shucked, chilled oysters.

Serves 4
· 6 oysters, shucked
· 1 shallot, diced
· 30g chorizo, small diced
· 30g roast red pepper,
  small diced
· 1 tsp. chopped parsley
· ½ tbsp. chipotle tabasco sauce
· 1 lemon cut into wedges

Preparation time: 15 mins

(See page 27 for techniques)

BAKED OYSTERS WITH CHORIZO AND PEPPERS

1. In a little oil, sweat off shallots over a medium heat for 1 minute, no colour. **2.** Add chorizo and cook for 2 minutes, then add peppers, parsley and tabasco and remove from heat. **3.** Turn your oven up to max. **4.** On a baking sheet, scrunch up a sheet of tin foil, place oysters on the foil, this will stop them from rolling around. **5.** Top each oyster with pepper and chorizo mix, pop into the oven for 5 minutes. **6.** Serve immediately with a lemon wedge.

'This dish can be prepared ahead of time or earlier in the day and finished in a hot oven before serving.'

TEMPURA OF OYSTERS

Serves 4
- 6 oysters, shucked
- 50ml refrigerated sparkling water
- plain flour

Preparation time: 10 mins
Cooking time: 5 mins

(See page 27 for techniques)

1. Pre-heat fryer to max. **2.** Remove oysters from shells, wipe shells clean with kitchen roll and arrange on your serving plate. **3.** Place approximately 50ml of sparkling water into a mixing bowl and add ½–1 tablespoon of flour, mix to form a batter consistency of double cream, don't over beat batter! **4.** Lightly dust oysters in flour, dip into batter, shaking off the excess batter and deep fry until golden. **5.** Serve with chilli jam (see page 72).

OYSTER ROCKEFELLER

Serves 4
- 6 oysters, shucked
- 1 clove garlic, minced
- 1 shallot, minced
- ½ tbsp. Pernod
- 100g fresh spinach leaves, washed
- 50g fresh breadcrumbs
- 1 rasher streaky bacon, diced small
- 1 lemon cut into wedges
- knob of butter
- chilli pepper

Preparation time: 10 mins
Cooking time: 8 mins

(See page 27 for techniques)

1. Remove oysters from shells, keep oysters and shells refrigerated. In a small frying pan, over a medium heat, sweat off shallots and garlic and 1 teaspoon of oil for 2 minutes. **2.** Add Pernod and spinach, sea salt and black pepper and a pinch of chilli pepper. **3.** Remove and leave to cool. **4.** For the topping, in a small frying pan, over a medium heat, add 1 teaspoon of butter, diced bacon, cook for 2 minutes then add breadcrumbs, cook out until golden. **5.** To finish, pre-heat oven to 225°C. **6.** Divide base mix between the six oyster shells, place oysters on top of the spinach mix, then sprinkle over breadcrumb topping. **7.** Bake in oven for 5–7 minutes and serve with a wedge of lemon.

Serves 4
· 12 poponcini peppers
· 200g white crab meat
· 1 hass avocado, finely chopped
· zest of ½ lime
· juice ½ lime
· 80g coriander, chopped
· 2 scallions, finely chopped
· pinch cayenne pepper
· pinch cumin powder
· sea salt and black pepper
· 100g crème fraiche
· 50g pea sprouts
· 50g rocket leaves

Alternative fish:
cooked lobster or prawns
Preparation time: 10 mins

STUFFED PEPPERS WITH CRAB AND AVOCADO

1. Mix all the ingredients except for the peppers, taste and adjust seasoning. **2.** Stuff peppers using a teaspoon, serve with pea sprouts and rocket leaves.

'Crab and avocado are a food marriage made in heaven! Throw in lime and a pinch of cayenne pepper and you have a taste explosion. Don't be fooled by the simplicity of the preparation of this dish as the combinations of fresh and light flavours make it an ideal starter or lunch dish. It could even make a starring appearance at a posh picnic as the peppers provide the perfect travel containers.'

Serves 4

For the bread:
- 500g strong white flour
- 7g sachet of fast action dried yeast
- 1 tsp. salt
- 4 tbsp. extra virgin olive oil
- up to 350ml lukewarm water
- ½ tsp. sugar
- 2 cloves garlic, minced
- 1 red onion, sliced
- 1 tbsp. rosemary, chopped
- 1 tbsp. anchovies, chopped
- oil for cooking

For the seaweed butter:
- 250g salted butter, soft
- 50g nori seaweed
- 1 glass white wine
- 1 sprig thyme
- 2 tbsp. parsley, chopped
- 2 cloves garlic, minced
- 2 shallots, sliced
- juice of 1 lemon
- zest of ½ lemon

Preparation time: 20 mins
Cooking time: 1 hour 45 mins

ANCHOVY, RED ONION AND ROSEMARY FOCACCIA AND SEAWEED BUTTER

1. In the bowl of an electric mixer with a dough hook attachment, proof the yeast by adding sugar to the water for 5 minutes until mix is foamy. **2.** Add flour and salt and 2 tablespoons of olive oil. Knead dough for 2–4 minutes; dough should be soft and slightly sticky. **3.** Form dough into a ball, transfer to an oiled bowl and turn to coat it with the oil, cover in cling film and set in a warm place until it doubles in size (for approximately 1 hour). **4.** Punch dough down, then press the dough evenly into an oiled baking sheet and let it rise, covered loosely in a warm place, until almost doubled in bulk. **5.** While dough is rising, cook onions in 1 tablespoon of olive oil for 5 minutes with sea salt. Add rosemary, garlic and anchovies then set aside. **6.** Heat oven to 200°C. **7.** Spread onion and anchovy mixture over the dough, gently press your fingers into the dough and drizzle with a little olive oil, sprinkle with sea salt flakes and fresh parmesan (optional). **8.** Bake for 30 minutes approximately (until golden). Leave to cool, serve cut or torn into squares.

SEAWEED BUTTER

1. Over medium heat, in a small saucepan, add wine, seaweed, thyme, garlic and shallots, cook until liquid has almost evaporated. **2.** Transfer into a food processor and process until smooth. Leave to cool and add butter, parsley, and the juice and zest of half a lemon. **3.** Process until smooth, taste and add salt or lemon if needed. **4.** Wrap finished butter in cling film. If refrigerated, will keep for a week (can also be frozen). **5.** Serve butter at room temperature.

Serves 4

· 300g scallop meat, small diced (no roe)
· 1 plum tomato, small diced (no seeds)
· 1 tbsp. shallot, minced
· 1–2 long red chillies, finely chopped
· 1 ripe avocado, small diced
· zest of 1 lime
· 50–75ml lime juice
· ½ tbsp. ground cumin
· 100g coriander, chopped

Alternative fish:
salmon or mackerel
Preparation time: 15 mins

SCALLOP CEVICHE

1. Combine all ingredients, season with sea salt to taste and serve with crostinis and lettuce cups.

'People who fret about these things have argued for years about the origins of ceviche. Some believe the dish, made typically from fresh raw fish, originated in Peru while others credit the Spanish for its creation. Frankly, where it came from is irrelevant as once you have tasted its plethora of flavours and textures you won't care either. It's a beautiful little gem, best enjoyed shared with friends and something fizzy chilled on a summer's afternoon.'

Makes 1 × 250ml jar

· 150g mackerel fillets
  (season with coarse sea salt
  and leave overnight)
· 1 tbsp. carrot, thinly sliced
· 1 tbsp. cucumber, thinly sliced
· 1 tbsp. shallots, thinly sliced
· 1 tsp. ginger, thinly sliced
· chilli flakes
· 50ml rice vinegar and 50ml
  mirin, mixed together

Alternative fish: herring,
bass or bream
Preparation time: 10 mins

(See page 27 for techniques)

JAPANESE PICKLED MACKEREL

1. Season vegetables with a few chilli flakes. **2.** Cut mackerel diagonally into strips 2cm long. Mix with vegetables. **3.** Pack into sterilised preserving jar, top up with vinegar and mirin. **4.** Seal and refrigerate for 1 week before opening. **5.** Serve with lettuce cups or focaccia crisps (see page 189).

'If you want to impress your friends with your knowledge of global culinary jargon, in Japanese this dish is known as Shime Saba. To get the best out of it make sure you use the freshest mackerel you can source as this fish quickly loses flavour if kept too long. Once made, pop this dish in the fridge for a week to allow it to develop properly but trust me, it's a treat worth waiting for!'

Serves 4

· 400g salmon fillet
  (no skin, no bones)
· 30g capers, rinsed repeatedly
  and squeezed dry
· 50g finely chopped smoked
  salmon (optional)
· 1 tbsp. chopped tarragon
· 1 tbsp. chopped chives
· 300g clarified butter
· pinch of cayenne pepper

Cucumber pickle:
· ½ cucumber
· rice vinegar

Alternative fish: brown shrimp,
salt cod or smoked mackerel
Preparation time: 10 mins
Cooking time: 10 mins

(See page 27 for techniques)

POTTED SALMON

1. Season salmon fillet with sea salt and black pepper.
2. Pop into a hot oven and cook for 7–10 minutes, depending on thickness of the salmon. **3.** Insert the tip of a knife into the thickest part of the salmon to check if cooked, if the salmon is cooked the flesh will flake apart easily. **4.** Flake cooked salmon into a mixing bowl, add chopped capers, smoked salmon, herbs and mix. Spoon the salmon into buttered ramekins, lightly press, cover with warm clarified butter and refrigerate. **5.** Remove from fridge 10 minutes before serving. Serve with melba toast and cucumber pickle.

CUCUMBER PICKLE

1. Take half a cucumber and cut in half again lengthways and slice diagonally, lightly salt and drizzle with rice vinegar.

TO CLARIFY BUTTER

1. Microwave butter until completely melted but don't boil. Skim off crusty top and pour off golden butter leaving cloudy substance at the bottom.

'This an economical dish as you can use up any salmon trim you may have.'

Serves 6
- 400g salt cod
- 100g mashed potato
- milk for poaching
- 1 bay leaf
- 75ml rapeseed oil or olive oil
- 100g shallots, finely chopped
- 3 cloves garlic, minced
- 200ml double cream
- juice of 1 lemon
- pinch of cayenne pepper

Preparation time: 1 day
Cooking time: 25mins

Home salted cod:
- 500g cod
- 1 level tbsp. coarse sea salt
- ½ tbsp. granulated sugar
- ¼ tsp. cracked black pepper
- 1 sprig fresh thyme,
  chopped fine

Alternative fish: conger eel, ling,
coley or pollock
Variation: smoked sea salt
Preparation time: 12 hours

(See page 27 for techniques)

BRANDADE

1. Soak salt cod in water for 6 hours, change water every 2 hours. **2.** Put salted cod in a saucepan, cover with milk and bay leaf. **3.** Bring to a simmer and then remove from the heat, cover and leave to stand for 20 minutes, then drain and flake the fish. **4.** Put a small saucepan over medium heat, add oil, shallot and garlic and cook until soft. **5.** Add the cream, bring to a simmer, add mash and salt cod. Blend salt cod and cream mixture until smooth and creamy. **6.** Add lemon juice and cayenne to taste.

HOME SALTED COD

1. Mix all of the ingredients. Rub into the fish. Put in a plastic bag to seal. **2.** Leave in the fridge for 12 hours, turning from time to time. Wipe the fish down and leave to dry on a rack where the air can circulate around it. **3.** Wrap in cling film and use as needed. **4.** Will keep for 1–2 weeks.

Serves 4
- 55ml buttermilk
- 50g smoked salmon, finely diced
- 50g chives, finely chopped
- 200g plain flour
- 2 tbsp. baking powder
- ¾ tsp. salt
- pinch of cracked black pepper
- 75g chilled unsalted butter, small cubes
- 1 large egg, beaten to blend (for glaze)

For the wasabi cream:
- 100ml clotted cream
- juice of ½ lemon
- zest of ½ lemon
- 2 tsp. wasabi powder
- 2 tbsp. chopped dill

Preparation time: 15 mins
Cooking time: 25 mins

SMOKED SALMON AND CHIVE SCONES WITH DILL AND WASABI CREAM

1. Pre-heat oven to 180°C. **2.** Mix flour, baking powder, salt and pepper in a large bowl. **3.** Add butter and with your fingers, work butter into flour until it resembles a fine breadcrumb. **4.** Then add smoked salmon, chives and buttermilk, lightly work until dough forms (don't overwork). **5.** Turn dough onto a floured surface, press out into a 7 inch round about half an inch thick. Using cutter, cut into rounds or cut freestyle with a sharp knife. **6.** Transfer onto a baking sheet. Brush tops with egg and bake until golden (approximately 20 minutes). **7.** Cool on rack and serve slightly warm with wasabi cream.

WASABI CREAM

1. In a small bowl, mix wasabi and lemon juice. **2.** Add dill and half of the cream. **3.** Mix well then gently mix in the remaining cream. **4.** Refrigerate for 20 minutes then serve.

STARTERS

Serves 4
· 4 boneless smoked
  herring fillets
· 400g baked beetroot,
  (skinned and cut into quarters)
· 1 Granny Smith apple, peeled
  and cut into strips
· 160g watercress
· olive oil or rapeseed oil
· balsamic vinegar
· sea salt and black pepper

Horseradish cream:
· 200ml sour cream
· 50g grated fresh horseradish
· 1 tbsp. chopped dill
· 1 tbsp. chopped chives
Mix together all of the above

Alternative fish: hot smoked
salmon or smoked mackerel
Preparation time: 10 mins
Cooking time: 5 mins

(See page 27 for techniques)

SMOKED HERRINGS WITH BEETROOT AND WATERCRESS SALAD AND HORSERADISH CREAM

1. Grill herrings under a hot grill for 4–6 minutes. Turn off grill and leave herrings to cook while you arrange the salad.
2. Season beetroot with sea salt and black pepper and drizzle with a little oil and balsamic vinegar, divide between the four plates, drizzle horseradish cream between the beetroot on the plates and sprinkle over watercress and apple. Finally top with warm smoked herring and serve.

'Beetroot tends to get a bad rap because most of us were forced to eat that pickled stuff out of jars with salads festooned with tinned pink meat when we were kids. However, prepare to look at fresh baked beetroot in a whole new light when you see how it complements the smoky earthiness of herrings – especially when it is ably supported by its deceptively punchy little garden friend – fresh horseradish. Not only is this dish packed with flavour and texture but it is also a visual treat of strong colours guaranteed to make your diners sit up and take notice.'

Serves 4

- 1 packet wonton wrappers
- 1 cooked lobster
- 100g white fish (cod, hake, whiting etc.)
- 1 scallion, minced
- 1 tsp. ginger, minced
- ¼ lime zest
- 1 tbsp. chopped coriander
- 1 tsp. sesame oil
- 1 egg, ½ for egg wash

For the broth:
- 1 litre chicken stock
- lobster shells
- 1 onion, chopped
- 1 knob ginger, chopped
- 4 cloves garlic, crushed
- 1 tbsp. coriander stalks
- 2 lemongrass, crushed
- 1 tbsp. tomato purée
- 2 limes, juiced
- 2 lime leaves
- 1 tbsp. curry powder
- fish sauce

For the garnish:
- 1 long red chilli, finely sliced
- 2 scallions, finely sliced
- 100g spinach leaves
- 50g beansprouts
- 4 tbsp. coriander, chopped

Alternative fish: prawn or crab
Preparation time: 20 mins
Cooking time: 1 hour

(See page 27 for techniques)

LOBSTER WONTONS WITH HOT 'N' SOUR BROTH

1. Place a large pot of seasoned water over a high heat and bring to the boil. **2.** While the water is coming to the boil add whitefish, scallion, ginger, lime zest, coriander and sesame oil to a food processor and process for 1 minute. **3.** Season with sea salt and set aside. **4.** Split lobster in half with sharp knife and remove tail meat. With the back of your knife, crack open claws and remove meat. Retain all lobster shells to make broth. Roughly chop down lobster meat and mix with the processed white fish. **5.** Lay out wonton wrappers side by side, 12 in total, place a 'marble' sized ball of the filling in the centre of each wonton wrapper, brush sides with egg wash and fold in half to make a triangle, squeeze sides together, try not to get any air trapped inside. Repeat on the rest of the wonton wrappers. **6.** Pop wontons into boiling water and cook for 4–5 minutes, strain, lay side by side on an oiled tray to cool.

HOT AND SOUR BROTH

1. In a large pot, over medium to high heat, add shells, onion, garlic, ginger, lemongrass and a drizzle of oil, cook for 5–10 minutes until veg just starts to colour. **2.** Then add tomato purée, lime leaves, curry powder, coriander stalks and cook for further a 3 minutes. **3.** Add stock and cook for 25 minutes on a low simmer. **4.** Strain then season with fish sauce and add fresh lime juice.

GARNISH

1. To finish, divide garnish between 4 warm soup bowls. Bring broth to the boil then add wontons to broth and bring back to the boil. **2.** Ladle broth into bowls, spoon 3 wontons per portion into broth and garnish and serve.

Serves 4

· 400g mixed seafood,
prawn meat, scallops, cod,
salmon etc. (no skin or bones)
· 1–2 tsp. Thai green curry paste,
more if you like it hot!
· 25g fresh coriander, chopped
· ½ bunch scallions, finely
chopped
· 100g fine egg noodles
(follow cooking instructions),
cooked and dried
· 1 egg yolk

Mango salsa:
· 1 large ripe mango, diced
· ½ red chilli, finely diced
· 15g coriander, finely chopped
· 2 scallions, finely diced
· fish sauce
· 1 tsp. pickled ginger, finely diced
· zest of ½ lime
· juice of 1 lime

Preparation time: 20 mins
Cooking time: 5 mins

ASIAN NOODLE CAKES WITH MANGO SALSA

1. Take 100g of the seafood and cut into small dice (½ cm).
2. Transfer into a large bowl, then add coriander and
scallions. Season with sea salt and black pepper. **3.** In a food
processor, blitz the rest of the seafood with curry paste, egg,
sea salt and black pepper. Add the processed seafood to the
diced seafood and mix. This is the base of your fish cakes.
4. Mould into 8 small equally sized patties. **5.** Roll patties
in cooked egg noodles, squeezing noodles into the cakes.
6. Pre-heat fryer to 160°C. **7.** Fry noodle cakes until light
golden colour and lift fry basket for 1 minute and then
re-fry until golden. **8.** Serve with mango salsa.

MANGO SALSA
1. Mix all of the ingredients together and season with
a little Thai fish sauce. **2.** This can be made the day before.
Keep refrigerated.

Serves 4

· 300g mixed fish (salmon, cod, hake etc. no skin or bones)
· 150g shellfish (prawns, scallops, crab, chopped)
· 1 egg
· 50g scallions, chopped
· 50g coriander, chopped
· 1 lime zest
· 1 tbsp. Cajun spice
· knob of butter
· 2 tbsp. plain flour

Guacamole:

· 2 'hass' avocadoes, quartered, pitted and peeled
· 75g chopped coriander
· 1 shallot, minced
· 1 chilli, minced
· 1 clove garlic, minced
· 1 lime, juiced
· sea salt

Preparation time: 15 mins
Cooking time: 8 mins

SANTA FE FISHCAKES WITH GUACAMOLE

1. In a food processor, place 300g mixed fish, cajun spice, sea salt, egg and process until smooth, then add coriander, scallions, zest and shellfish and gently pulse until just mixed. **2.** Divide fishcake mix and mould into 8 equal sized patties. **3.** Refrigerate for 10 minutes. **4.** Place 2 large non-stick frying pans over high heat, add a drizzle of oil and a knob of butter to each pan. **5.** Lightly dust patties with flour. When butter in frying pan starts to brown, add fishcakes, colour golden, then reduce heat to medium. Turn and colour the other side for 5 minutes. **6.** Cut into the centre of one of the cakes to make sure it is cooked through. **7.** Serve with salad and guacamole.

GUACAMOLE

1. Put all ingredients into a bowl and mash with a fork until smooth, taste and adjust seasoning.

Serves 8–10

- 500g mixed seafood (mussels, cockles, prawns, cod, salmon etc.)
- 1 onion, diced
- 2 ribs of celery, diced
- 1 leek, diced
- 200g celeriac, peeled and diced
- 1 bulb fennel
- 400g potatoes, peeled and diced
- 2 bay leaves
- 1 sprig thyme
- 4 litres stock, fish or chicken
- 500ml double cream
- 100g butter
- chopped parsley
- cayenne pepper
- croutons

Preparation time: 15 mins
Cooking time: 40 mins

SEAFOOD CHOWDER

1. In a large pot, over a medium heat, add butter, onions, bay and thyme. Season and gently sweat off for 5 minutes until onions are soft but no colour. **2.** Add fennel and celery and cook for another 3 minutes, then add celeriac, potato and leeks and bring stock to the boil. Taste for seasoning and cook out for 25 minutes. **3.** Remove from the heat. **4.** With a hand blender gently pulse blend the soup, just enough to thicken it, but not enough to purée it, put back on the heat and add seafood (seafood should be diced, no shells, bones or skin). **5.** Bring to a simmer and add cream. **6.** Adjust seasoning with sea salt and a good pinch of cayenne pepper. **7.** Pour into warm bowls and top with croutons and parsley.

'Chowder is just a fancy word for stew or thickened soup and there is no more welcoming dish on a cold night when you have staggered in from the wind and rain. It will positively warm you from the inside out. Every chef has their own way of preparing seafood chowder and I recommend you tailor this straightforward recipe to your particular tastes to make it your own. Invest a little bit of time and effort in this and you will be rewarded with a soup that is waiting to give you a warm hug on a winter's night!'

Serves 4

· 240g tiger prawns, peeled and deveined
· 1 dried habanero chilli, chopped (no seeds) or ½ tsp. chilli flakes
· 4 cloves garlic, minced
· 1 lemon zested and juiced
· 80g chopped parsley
· 1 tsp. sweet paprika
· pinch of fresh chopped thyme
· 100g roast red pepper, sliced
· 50ml rapeseed oil
· 8 slices of focaccia

Alternative fish: langoustine, monkfish, squid
Preparation time: 10mins
Cooking time: 10mins

PIRI PIRI PRAWNS WITH PEPPERS AND BRUSCHETTA

1. In a mixing bowl, combine chillies, prawns, paprika, zest, thyme and garlic. Season with sea salt and black pepper, mix and set aside. **2.** Heat a large frying pan over a high heat and fry prawns for 30 seconds on each side. Add peppers, parsley, lemon juice and oil. Serve with grilled focaccia.

'Piri Piri is a Portuguese chilli sauce consisting of dried habaneros, paprika, lemon and garlic packing the punch of a powerful pugilist! These prawns will awaken even the most jaded taste buds and although it takes only minutes to cook them, my strong advice is to make extra because everyone will want second helpings. They are sunshine in a bowl and are the perfect finger food if you are entertaining or a lighter alternative for Sunday lunch in summer.'

Serves 4
· 250g squid
· 1 egg white

Flour mix:
· 150g rice flour
· 150g potato flour
· 50g milk powder
Mix all of the above together

Chilli jam:
· 100ml of olive oil
· 1 400g tin chopped tomatoes
· 2 tbsp. tomato purée
· 1 large white onion,
  chopped fine
· 1 tbsp. fresh ginger, minced
· 3 cloves garlic, minced
· 1 red chilli, chopped
  (seeds in)
· 2 black cardamom
· 2 green cardamom
· ½ tsp. turmeric
· 1 tbsp. curry powder
· ½ tbsp. garam masala
· ¼ tsp. black mustard seeds
· 1 bay leaf
· 2 inch piece of cassia bark
· 1 tbsp. grated palm sugar
· 1 tsp. tamarind concentrate
· fish sauce to taste
· cayenne pepper, a pinch
  (or a few if you like it hot)

Alternative fish: monkfish,
gurnard, sole or prawns
Preparation time: 10 mins
Cooking time: 5 mins

SALT 'N' CHILLI SQUID

1. Get fishmonger to prep squid, cut into small 2 inch squares or rings. Coat in egg white, shake off all the excess, coat in flour mix and set aside. You should do this 15 minutes before frying. **2.** Fry in deep fryer at highest setting until lightly golden and remove. Shake off excess oil and season with sea salt and cayenne pepper. **3.** Serve with chilli jam and napa slaw (see page 183).

CHILLI JAM

1. Toast off whole spices and grind in a pestle and mortar. **2.** Cook off vegetables over a medium heat in 100ml of oil and teaspoon of sea salt. **3.** Add all the spices and tomato purée and cook out for 5 minutes. Then add chopped tomatoes, sugar and tamarind. **4.** Cook out on low heat for 20 minutes. Then 'mouli' or process. Better result if put through a potato 'mouli' or 'ricer'. **5.** Adjust seasoning with fish sauce and add more sugar or tamarind to adjust sweet and sourness. **6.** Store in fridge and this will keep for a week.

Serves 4
· 4 × 150g boneless, skinless
  salmon steaks
· olive oil or rapeseed oil
· butter
· sea salt and black pepper
· Japanese pickled vegetables

Teriyaki sauce:
· 75ml Kikkoman soy
· 75ml mirin (Japanese sweet
  rice wine) or sherry
· 2 tbsp. honey
· 1 tsp. minced ginger
· 1 tsp. minced garlic
Mix together all of the above

Pickle:
· ¼ tsp. Szechuan peppercorns,
  toasted and crushed
· 1 tbsp. peanut oil or ½ tbsp.
  sesame oil
· ½ tsp. ginger, minced
· 25ml rice vinegar
· 25g yellow rock sugar
  or caster sugar

Japanese pickled vegetables:
· ½ cucumber (no skin, no seeds)
· 50g red radish
· 50g white radish
· ½ red chilli (no seeds)
· 50g pea shoots

Alternative fish: mackerel,
eel or shark
Preparation time: 15 mins
Cooking time: 10 mins

(See page 27 for techniques)

TERIYAKI SALMON WITH JAPANESE PICKLED VEGETABLES

1. Lightly season salmon with sea salt and pepper.
2. In a large non-stick frying pan, over a high heat, add a drizzle of oil and a teaspoon of butter. When the butter starts to turn brown, add the salmon steaks, lightly colour both sides. **3.** Add the teriyaki sauce, pop under hot grill, continually coating and basting until fish is cooked and teriyaki is reduced and slightly sticky. **4.** Serve immediately with Japanese pickled vegetables.

JAPANESE PICKLED VEGETABLES

1. In a pan, over medium heat in a little vegetable oil, gently fry ginger, then add vinegar and sugar. Heat until sugar dissolves, then add peppercorns and peanut oil. Leave to cool. **2.** Cut cucumber, radish and chilli into fine strips or circles and season with sea salt. Add pea shoots and dress with pickle.

Serves 10–12
- 1kg organic salmon (skin on, scaled, skinned and boned)
- 150g coarse sea salt
- 150g demerara sugar
- 2 tsp. cracked black pepper
- 200g chopped dill
- ½ tsp. cinnamon

Dill sauce:
- 1 tbsp. caster sugar
- 75g Dijon mustard
- ½ tbsp. red wine vinegar
- 175g rapeseed oil or olive oil
- 50g chopped dill

Garnish:
- 100g cooked beetroot
- 100g seasoned avocado

Preparation time: 2 days

(See page 27 for techniques)

GRAVLAX WITH BEETROOT, AVOCADO AND DILL SAUCE

1. Mix marinade together and rub into the flesh. Place in a plastic bag and refrigerate for 48 hours, turning from time to time, draining off excess liquid as you turn. **2.** After 48 hours, wipe off excess marinade, pat dry and lightly sprinkle with chopped dill. Store fillet skin side down, keep refrigerated for 1 week.

DILL SAUCE

1. Put all ingredients in a screw top jar and shake like crazy, then serve. **2.** To serve, slice gravlax into thin slices with a sharp knife, layer flat on a plate or platter. **3.** On top of the gravlax arrange some seasoned avocado and cooked beetroot; drizzle with dill sauce and serve with wheaten bread.

'It's hard to do gravlax for 4–6 people. 1 kg of fish should serve 10–12 people. Great for a party or just keep eating it all week! Gravlax means buried salmon.'

Serves 4
- 8 mackerel fillets
- 2 tbsp. honey

Smoke mix:
- 110g jasmine tea
- 100g sugar
- 100g rice (any variety)

Mango salad:
- 2 large mangoes, peeled and cut into thin strips
- 1 baby gem lettuce, shredded
- 1 bunch scallions, finely chopped
- 8 red radish, sliced
- 100g chopped coriander

Hot 'n' sour dressing:
- 4 long red chillies, deseeded and chopped
- 2 cloves garlic, minced
- 2 tbsp. grated palm sugar (jaggery)
- juice and zest of 1 lime
- 75ml fish sauce
- 25ml rice vinegar

Whisk together all of the above

Alternative fish: herring, bass, bream or sardines
Preparation time: 15 mins
Cooking time: 25 mins

(See page 27 for techniques)

TEA SMOKED MACKEREL WITH HOT 'N' SOUR MANGO SALAD

1. Brush mackerel fillets lightly with honey, season with salt and refrigerate for 2 hours before smoking.

TO SMOKE THE MACKEREL

1. Cut out a circle of foil about 20cm diameter and scrunch up the sides. Put the tea smoke mix into foil container, place it in the bottom of a wok, then place the rack over the top. Turn up the heat to full and once the mix starts smoking, add the fish. Cover with a lid and leave over heat for 3 mintues. Remove the wok from the heat. Allow the wok to cool and the smoke to slowly dissipate. To finish mackerel, pop under a hot grill on a non-stick tray for approximately 5 minutes until skin is crisp. **2.** Combine all the salad ingredients and dress with hot 'n' sour dressing. Put dressed salad in the centre of each plate and top with the smoked mackerel.

'You don't need a fancy smoker to achieve the delicate flavours in this dish. A combination of tin foil, a hot pan and a sense of adventure is all that is required. In fact you can experiment with different tea types and spices to tailor the taste to suit your palate as you will be amazed how this simple smoking technique adds a whole new dimension of flavour to this dish. The piquant mango salad also provides the perfect accompaniment to hot smoked salmon and smoked herrings so try different options and keep this wonderful dish on high rotation in your menu selection.'

LIGHT BITES

Serves 4

· 100g squid cut into 2cm pieces
  (get fishmonger to clean squid)
· 1 medium white onion,
  small dice
· 100g chorizo, small dice
· 300g risotto rice
· 1 glass white wine
· 1 litre of stock
  (fish or chicken)
· olive oil
· 75g grated parmesan

Smoked paprika butter:
· 1 tsp. lemon juice
· 50g butter (soft)
· ½ tsp. smoked paprika
· ¼ tsp. of chopped fresh
  rosemary

Alternative fish: prawns,
monkfish or clams
Preparation time: 10 mins
Cooking time: 30 mins

SQUID AND CHORIZO RISOTTO WITH SMOKED PAPRIKA BUTTER

1. Combine all ingredients for the paprika butter in a bowl, mix well and then refrigerate. **2.** Heat the stock in a separate saucepan. **3.** Heat 2 tablespoons of olive oil over a medium heat, add chorizo and onion, sea salt and black pepper, cook low and slow for 10 minutes until onions are soft and chorizo has rendered and released all its natural oils. **4.** Add the rice, cook for approximately 2–3 minutes then add wine and stir until the wine has totally evaporated. **5.** Then add stock a ladle at a time, stirring continuously, allow each ladle full of stock to be absorbed before adding the next. In approximately 15 minutes rice should simmer. Too high a heat will cook the rice too quickly on the outside and cause your risotto to taste 'grainy'. **6.** When you are down to your last 3–4 ladles of stock, taste your risotto, rice should be soft, but have a slight bite, all risottos differ so there is slightly more stock than you might need, it should have the consistency of a soft porridge. Add smoked paprika butter and parmesan, stir and remove from the heat and rest. Taste and adjust seasoning. **7.** While risotto is resting, place a frying pan over high heat, add 1 tablespoon of olive oil, season squid with sea salt and black pepper, carefully place into frying pan and sauté for 2–3 minutes. **8.** While squid is cooking, spoon risotto into 4 warm bowls, then top with sautéed squid and finish with a good sprinkle of gremolata (optional see page 178) or flat leaf parsley.

'Before cooking the squid, pat dry with kitchen roll, you want the squid to cook quickly, any moisture on the squid will cause it to stew, not fry.'

Serves 4
· 1 lemon cut into wedges
· 320g smoked salmon
· 4 free range eggs
· 100g rocket

Pancakes:
· butter for cooking
· 500g fresh mashed potatoes
  (room temperature)
· 4 egg yolks
· 2 egg whites, lightly whisked
· 4 tbsp. of plain flour, sieved
· 1 tbsp. chopped dill
· 3 tbsp. cream
· lemon oil (see page 180)

Alternative fish: smoked trout,
eel or mackerel
Preparation time: 15 mins
Cooking time: 10 mins

SMOKED SALMON POTATO PANCAKE WITH ROCKET AND SOFT BOILED EGG

1. Pre-heat oven to 220°C. **2.** To make pancakes, mix yolks, mash, dill and cream together in a large bowl, then add egg whites and flour, mix but don't overwork the pancake mix. Set aside. **3.** Bring a pot of water to the boil, add in whole eggs and set a timer for 7 minutes, remove and leave to rest for 2 minutes then peel. **4.** While eggs are cooking, place a large non-stick frying pan over a medium heat. Add a knob of butter. When butter just starts to turn brown, add a spoonful of pancake mix, mix should make 4 large pancakes in total. Shake pan so pancakes don't stick, then slide pan into oven for 2 minutes, then remove pan and turn pancakes and slide back into the oven and bake for a further 3 minutes. Pancakes should be golden on both sides. **5.** To serve, place warm pancakes onto plate, then a few leaves of rocket and a drizzle of lemon oil, followed by smoked salmon and topped with your soft-boiled egg, lemon wedge, sea salt and black pepper.

'The warm soft yolk and squeeze of lemon will have the same characteristics of Hollandaise sauce without the hassle of making it. If you crack your egg while it is cooling down it makes it a lot easier to peel.'

Serves 4
· 800g fresh mussels
· 1 bulb fennel, thinly sliced
· 1 small white onion,
  thinly sliced
· 4 cloves garlic, minced
· 1 bunch parsley, chopped
· 200ml white wine
· 800ml whipping cream

Alternative fish: clams or cockles
Preparation time: 15 mins
Cooking time: 8 mins

(See page 27 for techniques)

MUSSELS WITH WHITE WINE CREAM

1. Split all ingredients in half. **2.** Place 2 large pots over a high heat, each must have a tight fitting lid. **3.** When pots are smoking hot, quickly add wine, fennel, onions, garlic and mussels, replace lid and cook out for 3 minutes, pour off half the liquid then add cream. **4.** Replace lid and cook out for 3–5 minutes until all of the mussels are opened. **5.** Add chopped parsley, spoon mussels and sauce into bowls and serve with warm crusty bread.

'This is a signature dish in Mourne Seafood Bar which keeps seafood lovers coming back for more. I believe it is the very simplicity of this dish with its honest and complementary flavours that make it a superstar on our menu.

Remember the rules about cooking mussels – if they don't open, don't eat them. Work quickly and with confidence over a high heat and bring the mussels to the table in their pots just like we do. These guys don't need fancy window dressing – just a huge wodge of fresh crusty bread and enthusiastic guests commanded to eat with their fingers.'

Serves 4
· 4 × 150g shark steaks,
  2–3cm thick
· 50ml rapeseed oil
· 1 tbsp. Cajun spice
· 1 sprig rosemary, chopped
· 1 clove garlic, minced

Butterbean Niçoise:
· 100g cooked green beans
· 100g tinned butterbeans
· 100g cherry tomatoes, halved
· 50g black Niçoise olives, pitted
· 4 hard-boiled eggs, quartered
· 75g mixed leaves

Dressing:
· 100ml mayo (See page 174)
· 8 anchovies, minced
· 2 cloves garlic, minced
· ½ lemon juice
*Mix well or use a hand blender
to mix together*

Alternative fish: swordfish
or salmon
Preparation time: 15 mins
Cooking time: 15 mins

SEARED SHARK WITH BUTTERBEAN NIÇOISE SALAD

1. Combine oil, spice, rosemary and garlic, rub over shark steaks and marinate overnight. **2.** Over a high heat, place a large non-stick frying pan, season steaks with sea salt. When the pan starts to smoke, carefully put in the shark steaks, cook for 2 minutes on one side and 1 minute on the other side. **3.** Steak should be slightly pink in the middle, serve over butterbean Niçoise.

BUTTERBEAN NIÇOISE
1. Place all ingredients in a large bowl, season with sea salt and black pepper, add dressing mix and serve.

'You can substitute shark for swordfish or salmon. Shark is also a great fish to barbeque.'

Serves 4

· 400g plaice fillets (skin off)
· 1 egg white and 1 tbsp. cream
  mixed together

Spiced flour:
· 150g plain flour
· 2 tbsp. sesame seeds
· 1 tsp. chilli powder
· 2 tsp. garam marsala

Crab slaw:
· 100g pickled white crab meat
· ¼ bunch scallions, finely
  chopped
· 50g grated carrot
· 150g white cabbage,
  shredded fine
· ½ cup mayo
· ¼ tsp. cayenne pepper
· 1 tbsp. ketchup

Szechuan fries:
· 400g peeled potatoes, large
  Roosters or new season
  Maris Pipers
· 50g butter, soft
· 1 tbsp. Szechuan peppercorns
· 1 lime, zested
· 25g grated ginger
· 1 red chilli, minced (seeds in if
  you like it hot)
· 25g coriander, chopped fine
· 2 garlic cloves, minced

Alternative fish: brill,
whiting or sole
Preparation time: 20 mins
Cooking time: 10 mins

(See page 27 for techniques)

SPICY FRIED PLAICE WITH CRAB SLAW AND SZECHUAN FRIES

1. To make slaw, in a large bowl add carrot, white cabbage, scallions, season with sea salt and cayenne pepper to taste, leave in the bowl for 20 minutes. **2.** Drain off any excess moisture, then add the rest of the ingredients and adjust seasoning, keeps for up to 24 hours. **3.** Pre-heat fryer to 180°C. **4.** Cut your plaice fillets the size of your little finger, 1cm across. **5.** Dust plaice with flour mix, make sure every piece is covered, shake off excess flour and dip into egg and cream mix and again shake off excess liquid and back into the flour (this can be done up to 20 minutes before frying depending on the size of your fryer). **6.** Fry in either one or two batches, be careful not to overcrowd the fryer. **7.** Fry until golden (for 4–5 minutes), season with fine sea salt, drain on kitchen paper, serve with crab slaw and Szechuan fries.

SZECHUAN FRIES

1. Pre-heat fryer to 140°C. **2.** Cut potatoes into chips. Blanch chips in fryer, until they are cooked through and still pale in colour. **3.** Remove and set aside (this can be done ahead of time). **4.** Combine all other ingredients. **5.** To finish, turn fryer up to 180°C, fry chips until golden, drain on kitchen roll, then in a large bowl, toss chips in Szechuan butter mix, coating all the chips. Season with sea salt and serve.

Serves 4
· 1kg fresh cleaned mussels
· ½ bunch fresh coriander

Sauce:
· 1 tsp. turmeric
· 1 tsp. garam marsala
· 2 tbsp. curry powder
· 1 white onion, roughly chopped
· 1 knob ginger, grated
· 2 garlic cloves, grated
· 1 tin coconut milk
· 1 cup cream / 200ml
· oil for cooking

Alternative fish: clams
Preparation time: 15 mins
Cooking time: 10 mins

(See page 27 for techniques)

KORMA MUSSELS

1. In a food processor, process onion, ginger and garlic, then add curry powder, turmeric and garam marsala to form a paste, fry paste in a little oil, then add coconut milk and cream (can be made in advance). **2.** Place a large pot with a tight fitting lid on a high heat. Let pot get really hot, remove lid and add mussels and sauce. Replace the lid and cook for 5–7 minutes, shaking the pot occasionally. **3.** When all mussels are opened, they're done. **4.** Finish with chopped coriander and serve with warm, crusty bread.

'For best results, split recipe in half and cook in 2 pots as this will allow the mussels to open more easily. The key to cooking mussels – high heat and small amounts.'

Serves 4
· 400g queen scallops
· ½ basic risotto base
  (see page 186)
· 200g butternut squash,
  peeled and deseeded
· 50g butter
· 4 rashers smoky bacon
· sage leaves
· 75g parmesan, grated
· 500ml stock (fish or chicken)

Alternative fish: king scallops,
langoustine meat or monkfish
Preparation time: 20 mins
Cooking time: 10 mins

QUEEN SCALLOPS WITH BUTTERNUT RISOTTO, CRISPY BACON & SAGE

1. Pre-heat oven to 200°C. **2.** Place butternut squash and butter in a small roasting tray, season with sea salt and black pepper, wrap in foil and bake for 30–45 minutes (until squash is soft). Remove from oven, peel off foil and mash to a pulp, set aside. **3.** Grill bacon until crispy and cut or break into bite-sized pieces, set aside. **4.** Shallow fry sage leaves over medium-high heat until crispy, set aside. **5.** In a medium saucepan, add 200g squash pulp and 100ml stock, heat over medium heat, then add risotto base, and gently heat. Add stock as needed. The consistency should be that of soft porridge. **6.** Place a large frying pan over a high heat. Season scallops with sea salt and black pepper. Add a drizzle of oil plus a small knob of butter, once the butter turns nut brown, add scallops and colour golden, turn scallops and they are done. **7.** Add parmesan to risotto and spoon into warm bowls, top with scallops and sprinkle crispy bacon and sage to serve.

'You can get all components of this dish ready ahead of time and simply put them together at the last minute and serve.'

Serves 4

- 200g cooked shellfish
  (white crab, prawns, lobster)
- 1 red chilli, finely chopped
  (no seeds)
- 50g bulgar wheat
- 4 scallions, finely chopped
- 50g basil, shredded
- 1 cucumber, small dice
  (no seeds)
- 100g cherry tomatoes,
  small dice (no seeds)
- 1 lemon
- 2 limes
- 1 orange
- 50ml olive oil

Alternative fish: cooked
monkfish, cod or salmon
Preparation time: 1 hour

SHELLFISH TABOULEH

1. With a sharp knife, carefully remove the outside skin and pith of the lemon, lime and orange, then dice citrus fruit into 1cm dice, making sure you retain all of the juice and place into a large bowl. **2.** Then add bulgar wheat, ½ teaspoon of salt, some black pepper and olive oil and leave to soak for 1 hour. **3.** Season cucumber and tomatoes with sea salt and add them to the bulgar and citrus. **4.** Add all other ingredients to the bowl and toss together.

'You may be thinking "what the hell is tabouleh?" Well fear not – it is simply a traditional salad originating in the Middle East made of bulgar wheat and it's in a league of its own when it comes to both taste and nutrition.

Tabouleh tastes fresh the day that it is made – but if you let it sit overnight, the flavours have a chance to blend and it tastes even better. Many recipes tell you to cook the bulgar wheat before adding it to your salad but it has already been power-boiled before it is dried so putting into boiling water again I feel makes it too stiff and reduces its wonderful texture.

I prefer to simply soak the bulgar wheat in the dressing so that it absorbs the concentrated flavours and it keeps the finished salad from being too watery.'

Serves 4
· 400g smoked haddock,
   cut into 50g pieces
· 440g Arborio rice
· 1,200ml milk
· 1 tsp. ginger, grated
· 1 tsp. garlic, minced
· 1 bay leaf
· 1 glass white wine
· 1 onion, chopped
· 60g butter
· 50g parmesan
· 50g cooked green beans
· 4 boiled eggs, chopped
· 3 tbsp. mild curry powder
· chopped coriander

Alternative fish: smoked whiting
or smoked eel
Preparation time: 20 mins
Cooking time: 30 mins

KEDGEREE RISOTTO

1. In a large pot, add milk, 1 teaspoon grated ginger, 1 teaspoon minced garlic, curry powder, 1 bay leaf and lightly season. **2.** Add smoked fish. Over a medium heat, bring to the boil and remove from the heat. **3.** Strain, but retain poaching liquor, this will be your stock to make the risotto. **4.** In a medium saucepan, add 30g butter and onion, season and cook until onions are soft, 4–6 minutes, then add rice and wine. **5.** Cook until the wine has been absorbed by the rice. Then a ladle at a time, add the poaching liquor, stirring continuously until each ladle has been absorbed. Cook al dente (for 20 minutes approximately). **6.** Then add the rest of the butter and parmesan, should have the consistency of soft porridge. **7.** Spoon into warm bowls, top with flakes of warm smoked fish, green beans, chopped egg and sprinkle with fresh coriander.

Serves 4

· 400g cooked and peeled langoustines or tiger prawns
· 50g couscous
· 50g quinoa
· 50g broccoli florets (cooked)
· 50g soy beans or peas (use frozen, lightly blanched and cooked)
· 1 punnet pea sprouts or mustard cress
· 50g cucumber, small dice
· 1 bunch scallions, chopped finely
· 1 pomegranate (seeds and juice only)
· 30g coriander
· 1 lemon, zest and juice
· 1 lime, zest and juice
· 30g basil
· fish sauce to taste

Alternative fish: lobster, crab or smoked mackerel
Preparation time: 20 mins
Cooking time: 20 mins

PRAWN SUPER SALAD

1. Cook prawns in a large pot of boiling seasoned water, 3–6 minutes, remove. Strain and place prawns in ice water to cool quickly. Peel off shells and set aside. **2.** Follow manufacturer's instructions and cook couscous and quinoa and place both into a large bowl. **3.** Add scallions, broccoli, soy beans, cucumber and herbs. Lightly season, then add lemon and lime juice. Add ¼ of the grated zest, finally add pomegranate seeds and juice, prawns and pea shoots. **4.** Taste and adjust seasoning with zest and a little fish sauce, toss together and serve. **5.** Can be made a few hours in advance.

'Quinoa is a complete protein and contains all 8 of the essential amino acids and this salad is virtually fat free.'

Serves 4

· 400g mixed seafood
  (squid, hake, whitebait,
  prawns, plaice etc.)
· 100g flour
· 40g cornflour
· pinch of salt
· 1 egg yolk
· 90ml carbonated water (cold)
· 90ml beer (cold)
· sprig of rosemary
· oil for frying

Basil mayo:
· 2 egg yolks
· 50ml lemon juice and ¼ tsp.
  of zest
· 1 tsp. Dijon mustard
· 200ml light olive oil
· 1 bunch basil, leaves only

Tuscan fries
· 400g fries, either homemade
  or frozen
· 100g tapenade
· 100g parmesan
· 50g chopped parsley

Preparation time: 20 mins
Cooking time: 8 mins

FRITTO MISTO, BASIL MAYO AND TUSCAN FRIES

1. In a bowl, mix flour, cornflour and salt with a whisk, then add egg and beer, mix to make a paste, then add water to form a runny batter, don't overwork the batter. Cover and place in the fridge for 2 hours. **2.** Using clean oil, turn your deep fryer to max. As oil is heating, add a sprig of rosemary to perfume the oil, remove rosemary when oil reaches max temperature. **3.** Cut seafood into small even sized pieces, 4–5 pieces per portion, lightly dust seafood in flour and dip into the batter, shake off the excess batter and fry in small amounts, fish in batter will float to the surface therefore put a sieve on top of the fish to keep them under the oil, cook for 2–4 minutes depending on size. Remove and start another batch, you can keep batches warm in a medium to low heat oven until finished. **4.** Serve with basil mayo and Tuscan fries.

BASIL MAYO
1. Liquidise basil and oil together to make basil oil.
2. Then place egg yolk, lemon juice, zest, salt and pepper and Dijon in a food processor, start processor then slowly add oil in a steady stream until incorporated. **3.** If mayo is too thick, thin with a tablespoon of warm water. Keeps for 2–3 days refrigerated.

TUSCAN FRIES
1. Fry or oven bake fries until golden and crispy. **2.** Put the fries into a large bowl straight from the oven or fryer. **3.** Add parsley and tapenade, toss until fries are coated in tapenade, then serve and top with parmesan.

MAINS

Serves 4

· 4 × 200g turbot steaks
  on the bone (skin on)
· 100g cockles
· 4 rashers of bacon, cut in 2cm
  pieces
· 1 glass of white wine
· 50g rosemary
· butter
· oil
· 300ml whipping cream

Alternative fish: brill
or large plaice
Preparation time: 10 mins
Cooking time: 15 mins

(See page 27 for techniques)

TURBOT 'ON THE BONE' WITH BACON, COCKLES AND ROSEMARY CREAM

1. Pre-heat oven to 250°C. **2.** In a large frying pan or skillet, over a high heat, add drizzle of oil and bacon. Fry for 2–3 minutes. **3.** Then season turbot steaks with sea salt and black pepper and add to pan. **4.** Cook and seal fish on all sides for 2–3 minutes, pop into the oven for 6 minutes, then add cockles and wine. **5.** Continue to bake for 2–3 minutes until wine has evaporated, then add rosemary and whipping cream. **6.** Remove from oven, place pan over high heat, bring to the boil, remove from the heat and serve.

'Turbot is a flatfish found in the shallow inshore waters of both the Mediterranean and the Norwegian Seas. It has a gleaming flesh that retains its bright white appearance when cooked. Turbot needs to be treated with the respect it deserves. Given its meaty quality is responds well to oven baking and steaming and in this recipe it gets a bit of both to ensure its wonderful flavour and texture get to literally shine through. The cockles, white wine and cream elevate this dish to something very special and it looks exciting and delicious when plated up. My top tip for cooking turbot is to keep the skin on while cooking and remove prior to serving as it helps the fish stay moist.'

Serves 4
· 4 × 300g of whole John Dory
  (no head or fins)

Saffron and Broighter
Gold vinaigrette:
· 9 strands of saffron
· 4 shallots, chopped fine
· 4 cloves garlic, minced
· 1 sprig thyme
· 1 bay leaf
· 1 glass white wine
· 1 lemon, juiced
· 200ml stock (fish or chicken)
· 50ml Broighter Gold
  Rapeseed Oil
· 200g cherry tomatoes, halved
  and seasoned with sea salt
· 80g basil, chopped

Alternative fish: seabass,
seabream, sole or plaice
Preparation time: 10 mins
Cooking time: 12 mins

(See page 27 for techniques)

BAKED JOHN DORY WITH WARM SAFFRON AND 'BROIGHTER GOLD' VINAIGRETTE

1. Pre-heat oven to 225°C. **2.** Season John Dorys with sea salt and black pepper, drizzle with a little oil and place flat on a roasting tray or casserole dish. **3.** Pop into the oven for 7 minutes, then spoon over vinaigrette. Return to the oven for 2 minutes, remove and finish with fresh basil.

VINAIGRETTE

1. In a medium saucepan over a low heat add shallots, garlic, thyme, bay leaf and sea salt and black pepper. **2.** Cook for 4 minutes (until soft), then add wine and saffron, turn up the heat and reduce until almost evaporated, then add stock. **3.** Reduce stock by 3 quarters (50ml). **4.** Remove from heat and add cherry tomatoes and rapeseed oil. Add lemon juice, basil and set aside.

'The inspiration for this dish comes from the discovery of a hoard of ancient Irish treasure discovered in 1896 in Limavady of all places. Appropriately, the Iron Age treasures included a golden boat and believe me, when you try this dish for yourself you will feel like you have struck lucky! It is delicious and healthy as rapeseed oil is possibly the healthiest cooking oil you can buy as it has half the saturated fat of olive oil and is packed with omega-3, 6 and 9. Even John Dory is credited with having a name taken from the French for gilded – so in my book this dish is definitely a gold medal winner.'

Serves 4
· 4 whole pin hake
  (get fishmonger to prep fish,
  no scales, no fins, no head)
· rapeseed oil, just for drizzling
  or 4 tbsp.

Antiboise sauce:
· 2 tbsp. chopped black pitted
  olives (Niçoise)
· 4 ripe plum tomatoes,
  diced small (no seeds)
· 2 shallots, minced
· 2 cloves garlic, minced
· 1 glass white wine
· 1 lemon, juiced
· 100ml lemon oil (see page 180)
· 1 tbsp. shredded basil
· 1 tbsp. chopped tarragon

Alternative fish: bass, bream,
sole or plaice
Preparation time: 10 mins
Cooking time: 15 mins

(See page 27 for techniques)

ROAST PIN HAKE WITH ANTIBOISE SAUCE

1. Pre-heat oven to 225°C. **2.** Season pin hakes all over inside and out with sea salt and black pepper. **3.** Drizzle fish with rapeseed oil and place on a baking sheet. Roast fish for 10–12 minutes. **4.** To test when cooked, fish flesh should come away easily from the back bone. **5.** Serve with herb roast potatoes (see page 180).

ANTIBOISE SAUCE

1. In a small saucepan over a medium heat, cook shallots with a drizzle of oil, season. **2.** Add garlic, white wine and cook until almost evaporated. **3.** Then add tomatoes, season well with sea salt and black pepper, add olives, herbs and lemon oil, gently cook until tomatoes just start to turn soft. **4.** Add lemon juice and serve.

Serves 4
- 4 whole mackerel, gutted and fins cut off
- 400g baby potatoes

Citrus relish:
- 1 grapefruit
- 1 orange
- 1 lime
- 1 lemon
- 1 chilli, finely diced (no seeds)
- 1 tbsp. chopped chives
- ¼ tsp. ground cumin

Herb oil:
- 1 tbsp. thyme, chopped
- 1 tbsp. rosemary, chopped
- 3 cloves garlic, minced
- 4 tbsp. rapeseed oil

Simply mix all of these ingredients together

Alternative fish: bass, bream, herring or sardines
Preparation time: 20 mins
Cooking time: 12 mins

(See page 27 for techniques)

WHOLE MACKEREL WITH CITRUS RELISH AND HERB ROAST POTATOES

1. For the salsa, segment all the citrus fruit. **2.** To do this use a sharp knife to cut the top and bottom off the fruit. **3.** Carefully from the top to the bottom, remove the skin and pith, then cut in between the membrane, but not through the centre of the fruit. **4.** When all of the segments have been removed, squeeze the rest of the juice over segments. **5.** Mix segments with cumin, chilli and chives. Can be made the day before and refrigerated. **6.** Pre-heat oven to 225°C. **7.** For the potatoes, halve new potatoes, toss in a little rapeseed oil and season with sea salt and black pepper, pop into a roasting tray and roast until golden and cooked through. Once cooked, toss in half of the herb oil. **8.** Potatoes can be done ahead of time and reheated again when you are cooking the fish (8 minutes) in a hot oven and serve. **9.** Season mackerel with sea salt and black pepper, also season inside of the fish and rub with the rest of the herb oil. **10.** Bake for 10–12 minutes, spoon over citrus relish and serve with herb roasted potatoes and rocket and fennel salad (see page 182).

'Mackerel has the highest content of omega-3 of any fish.'

Serves 4

· 4 × 150g brill steaks
  (without skin)
· 300g risotto base
  (see page 186)
· 100g white crab meat
· 30g chervil and tarragon
· flour for dusting
· 1 egg + 4 tbsp. milk
  (mix to make egg wash)
· 100g fresh breadcrumbs
· knob of butter
· drizzle of rapeseed oil

Sauce vierge:
· 2 cloves garlic, minced
· 50g shallots, finely chopped
· 100g ripe tomatoes, diced
  (no seeds)
· 150ml extra virgin olive oil
· juice of ½ lemon
· 1 tbsp. chopped tarragon
· 6 coriander seeds, toasted
  and crushed

Alternative fish: salmon, cod,
hake, plaice or turbot
Preparation time: 20 mins
Cooking time: 12 mins

(See page 27 for techniques)

BRILL WITH CRAB RISOTTO CAKES AND SAUCE VIERGE

1. For the cakes, mix together your risotto base, crab meat, herbs and mould into 4 cakes, dust with flour, coat in egg wash and then cover in breadcrumbs, remould cakes ready for cooking. **2.** Pre-heat oven to 225°C. **3.** Season brill with sea salt and black pepper. **4.** Over a high heat, place 2 large non-stick pans, add a drizzle of oil and knob of butter. When the butter starts to brown, add 2 portions of brill along with 2 cakes to each pan. **5.** Cook until the cakes and brill are golden on one side, turn and place both pans in the oven for 4–5 minutes. **6.** Spoon warm sauce vierge onto warm plates, top with crab risotto cake and then brill, serve with green vegetables.

SAUCE VIERGE

1. For the sauce, put the shallots, coriander seeds, tomatoes, garlic and olive oil in a saucepan, season with sea salt and pepper and gently heat for 3 minutes. Add lemon juice and herbs just before serving.

· 100g mussels, cleaned
· 4 oysters, shucked
· 100g crab claws, cooked
  or whole prawns or both
· 400g assorted fish (salmon, cod,
  monkfish – no bones or skin)
· 4 plum tomatoes
· 1 bulb fennel, thinly sliced
· 4 tbsp. tomato sauce
  (alternative: use pasta sauce)
· 1 litre shellfish stock (see page
  166), fish and chicken stock will
  also work
· 400g cooked baby potatoes,
  cut in 2cm thick circles
· knob of butter

Gremolata:
· zest of 1 lemon (grated)
· 100g parsley, chopped
· 4 cloves garlic, minced
Mix all ingredients together

Preparation time: 15mins
Cooking time: 25mins

SEAFOOD CASSEROLE

1. Over a high heat, place 2 large non-stick frying pans (2 portions in each pan). **2.** Season assorted fish with sea salt and black pepper. **3.** Add drizzle of oil and a small knob of butter to each pan. When butter begins to brown, add assorted fish, colour until golden then turn fish. **4.** Add potatoes, tomatoes, fennel, season, then add all shellfish, stock and 2 tablespoons tomato sauce to each pan, place a lid or tin foil over each pan and cook over medium heat for 4 minutes. **5.** Remove lid, serve in warm bowls, finish with a drizzle of rapeseed oil, crusty bread and a sprinkle of gremolata.

· 4 × 150g halibut steaks
 (no bones or skin)

Spicy aubergine:
· 2 aubergines
· 1 red onion, diced
· 100g plum tomatoes, 2cm dice
 (no seeds)
· 4 anchovies, minced
· ½ habanero chilli, minced
 (no seeds)
· 4 cloves garlic, minced
· 50ml lemon oil (see page 180)
· 50g chopped basil

Alternative fish: salmon, hake,
cod, turbot or brill
Preparation time: 30 mins
Cooking time: 12 mins

(See page 27 for techniques)

HALIBUT WITH SPICY AUBERGINE AND SAFFRON MASH

1. Season halibut with sea salt and black pepper. Place large non-stick pan over high heat. **2.** Add drizzle of oil and knob of butter, once butter starts to turn brown add halibut, cook until golden, then turn and remove from heat, cover pan in tin foil and leave for 4 minutes. **3.** Remove foil and serve. Both aubergine and mash can be made ahead of time.

SPICY AUBERGINE

1. Pre-heat oven/grill to 250°C. **2.** Rub 1 aubergine with oil and bake/grill until aubergine is roasted all the way through and soft and mushy in the middle. **3.** Using a spoon, scoop and scrape the inside of the aubergine into a bowl, season and set aside. Discard the skin. **4.** Dice the remaining aubergine. **5.** Place large frying pan over a high heat with a drizzle of rapeseed oil, add red onions, season and cook for 2 minutes. **6.** Then add aubergine, sea salt and black pepper and another drizzle of oil, reduce heat slightly and cook for a further 5–8 minutes. **7.** Then add garlic, anchovies, chilli, tomatoes and season. Finally, add basil and aubergine purée. Taste and adjust seasoning and finish with lemon oil. See page 188 for saffron mash.

'Can be made ahead of time, keeps refrigerated for 2 days and heat in microwave or over low heat in a sauce pan.'

Serves 4

- 2 × 400–500g whole plaice
  (get fishmonger to fillet plaice,
  discard head, tail and skin.
  Reserve plaice bones for later.
  You need to have 8 fillets,
  approx. 60–80g each)

Pesto:
- 200g basil
- 100g flat parsley
- 100g parmesan cheese
- 50g pine nuts, toasted
- 4 cloves garlic, minced
- 200ml olive oil

Stuffing:
- 100g pesto
- 100g fresh breadcrumbs

Saffron baked potatoes:
- 500g baby potatoes, peeled and
  cut in 3cm thick circles
- 1 bulb fennel, halved and finely
  sliced
- 100g shallots, finely sliced
- bay leaf and thyme
- 2 cloves garlic, minced
- fish bones
- 20 saffron strands and 1 litre
  water (heat and infuse for
  20 minutes)
- 80g basil
- 100g tomatoes, deseeded and
  roughly chopped
- 100g butter

Alternative fish: lemon sole
or Dover sole
Preparation time: 20 mins
Cooking time: 40 mins

(See page 27 for techniques)

PESTO STUFFED PLAICE WITH SAFFRON BAKED POTATOES

1. Pre-heat oven, medium high at 180°C. **2.** In a large stainless roasting dish over a medium heat, add drizzle of oil, shallots, fennel, salt and pepper, and then add garlic, bay, thyme, potatoes and fish bones. **3.** Season with lots of salt and pepper, then add saffron and water. **4.** Bring to the boil, adjust seasoning (liquid should taste slightly salty). **5.** Add butter, wrap with foil, bake in oven for 30–40 minutes until potatoes are soft. **6.** Add tomatoes and basil just before serving.

PESTO

1. Put all of the ingredients in a blender or food processor and blend to a chunky paste.

FOR THE PLAICE

1. Add pesto to the breadcrumbs to make stuffing. **2.** Lay out plaice fillet, skinned side facing up, lightly season with sea salt and black pepper. **3.** Mould stuffing into small sausage shape and place at the smallest end of the fillet and roll to the large end, repeat 7 times. **4.** Place fish on a greased baking sheet and bake for 12–15 minutes in a medium to hot oven.

TO SERVE

1. Carefully remove fish bones from saffron potatoes and spoon into bowls. The brazing liquor from the potatoes makes a great sauce for the fish, then top with the plaice.

Serves 4
- 2 × 1.5lb lobsters (cooked)
- 4 cloves garlic
- 4 shallots
- 2 tbsp. Pernod
- 400g fresh spinach leaves
- 200g breadcrumbs
- 4 rashers bacon, diced small
- 50g chopped parsley
- pepper
- pinch chilli powder
- rapeseed oil

Béarnaise potatoes:
- 500g baby potatoes (new season Combers), cut into halves
- 75g minced shallots
- 50g chopped tarragon
- 50g chopped chervil
- 1 lemon, zest and juice
- 100g salted butter – local 'Abernethy Butter' works best

Alternative fish: oysters or scallops
Preparation time: 20 mins
Cooking time: 10 mins

(See page 27 for techniques)

LOBSTER ROCKEFELLER

1. Pre-heat the oven to 225°C. **2.** Follow the cooking demo for fresh lobster. Split cooked lobster, remove meat from tail, crack claws and remove meat. Take the 4 lobster halves, split the meat into 4 equal portions and set aside (don't discard lobster claw shells – these can be frozen and used for a stock or broth). **3.** Over a medium heat in a large saucepan add shallots, salt and pepper and a drizzle of oil, cook for 2 minutes. Then add the garlic, Pernod, spinach, salt and a pinch of chilli powder. Cook until spinach is just cooked, remove from the heat and set aside. **4.** In a large frying pan over a medium heat fry chopped bacon in 4 tablespoons of oil until crispy; then add the breadcrumbs stirring continuously. Finally add the parsley, remove from the heat and set aside. **5.** To assemble the lobsters place your 4 half shells on a baking sheet – then line the bottom of the shells with your spinach mix. Then layer in the cooked lobster in bite-sized pieces on top of the spinach. Finally top lobster with the breadcrumb and bacon mix. **6.** Place in the oven and cook for 8 minutes. **7.** Serve one half tail per person with Béarnaise potatoes.

BÉARNAISE POTATOES
1. Cook baby potatoes in salted water. **2.** Once potatoes are cooked strain and put back into a dry pan. Add all the other ingredients, cover with a lid and give them a good shake. **3.** Serve.

· 4 × 160g boneless salmon
  steaks (skin on)
· 1 bunch asparagus, halved
· 100g samphire
· 100g shelled peas
· butter
· lemon juice

Alternative fish: cod, hake
or haddock
Preparation time: 20 mins
Cooking time: 40 mins

(See page 27 for techniques)

ROAST FILLET OF SALMON WITH PEAS, ASPARAGUS, SAMPHIRE AND SMOKED SALMON GRATIN

1. Pre-heat oven to 250°C. **2.** Have a pot of water on a soft boil ready for cooking your veg. **3.** Place a large frying pan, or 2 medium fying pans, over a high heat. **4.** Season salmon steaks with lots of sea salt and black pepper. **5.** Add a little oil and a knob of butter to frying pan, once the butter starts to turn brown, add the salmon skin side down. Carefully colour the skin, then turn steaks over and place in the oven for 7 minutes. **6.** Once fish goes into the oven, place asparagus into boiling water, wait 2 minutes then add samphire, wait 2 more minutes, then add peas, 2 minutes more, drain, toss in sea salt, butter and lemon juice. Spoon vegetables onto plates and top with salmon. **7.** Serve smoked salmon gratin on the side (see page 187).

'Samphire is a sea vegetable that grows abundantly on our shorelines, it can be a bit one-dimensional, but works great mixed with asparagus and peas.'

Serves 4
· 4 large gurnard fillets
· 300g mussels (cleaned)
· olive oil
· 1 white onion, diced
· 1 leek, diced
· 1 courgette, diced
· 1 bulb fennel, diced
· 400g tin of white beans
  (rinsed and drained)
· bay leaf and sprig of thyme
· 1 glass white wine
· 2 plum tomatoes, chopped
  (no seeds)
· 250ml stock (fish or chicken)

Pistou:
· 5 cloves garlic, minced
· 60g grated parmesan
· 50ml olive oil
· 50g basil leaves
· 50g flat leaf parsley leaves

Alternative fish: mackerel, plaice,
whiting or salmon
Preparation time: 20 mins
Cooking time: 15 mins

(See page 27 for techniques)

GURNARD FILLETS WITH MUSSELS AND PISTOU BROTH

1. In a large pot over a medium heat, add onion, bay and thyme, fennel, and a drizzle of oil, sea salt and black pepper, cook for 8–12 minutes, there should be no colour but the onions will have softened. **2.** Then add leeks and courgettes and season, cook for 3–5 minutes, then add beans, tomatoes and stock and bring to the boil and set aside. **3.** Place a large pot with lid over a high heat, add mussels and wine and replace lid, cook until all mussels have opened, drain off cooking liquor through sieve and reserve the liquor, pick mussel meat from the shell and place into reserved cooking liquor. **4.** Add all the mussel meat and liquor into your pot with the vegetables and beans, bring to the boil and adjust seasoning. **5.** Season gurnard fillets on both sides with sea salt and cracked black pepper, drizzle with olive oil and place on a baking sheet, slide under a hot grill, skin side up and cook for 5 minutes, turn off grill, close oven door and rest fish for 3–4 minutes. **6.** While fish is resting, return bean and mussel broth to the boil, then add pistou. Remove from heat and spoon into 4 bowls then top with gurnard fillets and serve.

PISTOU
1. Process all ingredients until smooth.

Serves 4

· 4 whole Dover soles 300–400g
  each (get fishmonger to remove
  head, tail, fins and top skin)

Black bean dressing:
· 4 cloves garlic, minced
· ½ tsp. ginger, minced
· 2 tbsp. fermented Chinese black
  beans – rinsed, chopped and
  drained
· 50ml light soy sauce
· 2 tbsp. dry sherry
· 1 tbsp. lemon juice
· 1 tsp. caster sugar
· 4 tbsp. peanut oil
· 1 tbsp. coriander, chopped

Herb salad:
· 1 scallion, finely sliced
· 30g chervil
· 30g coriander
· 30g pea shoots
· 1 red chilli, finely sliced with
  no seeds

Alternative fish: sole,
plaice or brill
Preparation time: 15 mins
Cooking time: 15 mins

(See page 27 for techniques)

BAKED DOVER SOLE WITH BLACK BEAN DRESSING AND HERB SALAD

1. Pre-heat oven on the grill/oven setting to high.
2. Season Dover sole with plenty of sea salt and black pepper. Drizzle with olive oil on both sides. **3.** Place fish on baking sheets and pop under grill, skin side facing upwards, cook fish for 5–6 minutes. **4.** Remove from the grill, drizzle a little more olive oil over the top of the fish and baste with the cooking juices, pop fish back in the oven, but place on a lower shelf. **5.** Cook for 5–6 minutes, check fish, if you can separate fish from the centre bone, it's done! **6.** Once fish is cooked, turn off oven and open oven door, let fish rest in the oven for 2 minutes. **7.** Serve Dover sole on warm oval plates; pour any cooking juices from the sole into your black bean dressing. Mix and spoon over the sole, then top sole with herb salad.

FOR THE DRESSING

1. Place saucepan over a medium to high heat. Add a drizzle of oil and fry ginger and garlic for one minute. **2.** As the garlic and ginger just starts to brown, add black beans and fry for one minute. **3.** Then add all other ingredients, except for the coriander, bring to a simmer, taste, adjust the balance of the lemon and the sugar if needed. **4.** Set aside to cool. **5.** Once cooled add the coriander. Keep dressing at room temperature until needed.

FOR THE SALAD

1. Pick coriander, chervil and pea shoots into small pieces. Mix in a small bowl with scallions and chilli and set aside.

'You can find Chinese black beans at any Asian supermarket.'

Serves 4

· 400g mixed seafood
  (prawns, cod, salmon, hake
  cut into 3cm pieces)
· 200g mussels, clams
  or cockles, cleaned
· 1 tbsp. Madras curry powder
· 1 red pepper, sliced
· 2 bok choy, quartered
  and washed
· 2 plum tomatoes, roughly
  chopped (no seeds)
· 1 white onion, diced
· 2 cloves garlic, minced
· 1 tsp. ginger, grated
· 1 red chilli, finely sliced
· 1 tsp. ground coriander
· 1 tsp. ground cumin
· 1 tsp. garam masala
· pinch of turmeric
· 2 tbsp. tomato purée
· 400ml coconut milk
· 50g chopped coriander
· 50ml stock (fish or chicken)
· ½ tsp. dark brown sugar
· 1 lime, juiced
· 4 scallions, sliced
· fish sauce to season
· 50g butter

Preparation time: 25 mins
Cooking time: 25 mins

SEAFOOD CURRY

1. In a large bowl, add mixed seafood, 1 tablespoon Madras curry powder, half a teaspoon of grated ginger, 1 clove of minced garlic and enough olive oil to coat the fish, mix and set aside. **2.** For the curry base, in a saucepan over a medium/low heat, add onions, 50g butter, sea salt and black pepper. Cook for 10–15 minutes, until soft but do not colour, then add the rest of the ginger, garlic and chilli. **3.** Cook out for 2 minutes, stir in spice and cook for 1 minute, add tomato purée and sugar, cook for 2 more minutes, then add coconut milk, bring to a simmer and set aside. **4.** In a large deep frying pan or 2 regular frying pans, place over a high heat, season the marinated seafood with sea salt and black pepper, carefully place the larger pieces of fish in first. **5.** Add all the fish, then add in the shellfish and lastly prawns and peppers, bok choy, tomatoes and season. **6.** Add stock and cook over a high heat until mussels just start to open, then add curry base, scallions and coriander, bring to the boil, taste, add lime juice and adjust seasoning with a little fish sauce. Serve with rice or naan bread.

Serves 4

· 4 whole gurnard
  (get fishmonger to prep
  gurnard, no head, gutted,
  no fins and skinned)
· 12 rashers of dry cured streaky
  bacon
· 12 sage leaves

Velouté sauce:
· 4 shallots
· 4 garlic cloves
· 1 sprig thyme
· 1 bay leaf
· 150g white fish bones – trim
  from gurnard is perfect
· 1 glass white wine
· 20g parsley stalks
· 20g chopped chives
· 200ml whipping cream

Alternative fish: small monkfish
tails or pin hake
Preparation time: 20 mins
Cooking time: 15 mins

(See page 27 for techniques)

BAKED WHOLE GURNARD WITH BACON AND SAGE SERVED WITH HERB VELOUTÉ SAUCE

1. Pre-heat oven to 250°C. **2.** Trim gurnards so that they are evenly sized. Any trim can be used in the herb velouté sauce. **3.** Lightly season gurnard with salt and pepper, arrange 3 sage leaves along the top of each gurnard, then carefully wrap tightly in bacon. Place on an oiled baking sheet. Bake for 10–12 mins until bacon is crispy. **4.** Serve with herb velouté as below.

VELOUTÉ SAUCE
1. Over a medium heat add the shallots, fish bones, garlic, bay, thyme, parsley, salt, pepper and a drizzle of oil to a saucepan. Cook for 5 mins, there should be no colouring. **2.** Then add the white wine and cook until the wine has evaporated. **3.** Add 150ml of water and cook until water has almost evaporated. **4.** Add the cream, bring to the boil and simmer for 3 mins. Strain sauce into a clean pan. **5.** This can be made and refrigerated ahead of time. To finish the sauce bring to the boil and finish with chives and parsley.

Serves 4
- 4 × 140–160g hake fillets
- 80ml rapeseed oil
- butter
- 400g cooked lentils
- 100g fresh shredded spinach leaf
- 8 scallions, finely chopped
- 4 plum tomatoes, diced and seeded
- 200g cooked diced potatoes
- 60g coriander, chopped
- 4 tsp. panang curry paste
- 100ml stock (fish or chicken)
- juice and zest of 1 lime
- fish sauce to season
- sea salt
- black pepper

Crispy green beans:
- 24 green beans 'topped and tailed'
- 100g plain flour, sieved
- 200ml sparkling water
- sea salt
- black pepper

Alternative fish: salmon, cod or haddock
Preparation time: 20 mins
Cooking time: 10 mins

(See page 27 for techniques)

PAN FRIED HAKE WITH CHILLI LIME LENTILS

1. In a large saucepan over a medium heat fry the panang paste for 2 minutes, then add scallions, tomatoes, potatoes and lentils, season with sea salt and black pepper and cook for a further minute. **2.** Then add stock and bring to the boil. Add the coriander, spinach, lime juice and zest. Season with fish sauce and set aside. **3.** Pre-heat the oven to max. **4.** Place a large non-stick frying pan over a high heat. Season the hake on both sides with sea salt and black pepper, add a drizzle of oil to the pan and a small knob of butter, when the butter turns brown, quickly add in the fish skin side down. Shake pan to prevent fish from sticking. **5.** Cook the fish until the skin is golden and carefully turn. Slide fish into the oven for 4–6 mins. **6.** While the fish is in the oven, reheat the lentils adding a little rapeseed oil. Spoon into warm bowls then top with the hake. Serve with crispy green beans.

CRISPY GREEN BEANS

1. Pre-heat deep fat fryer to 180°C. **2.** Place flour into a bowl; add the water a little at a time. The batter should resemble the consistency of double cream. Do not over mix the batter. **3.** Then quickly dip green beans in batter and carefully drop into the fryer, cook until golden. **4.** Remove from the fryer and drain on kitchen paper. **5.** Season with sea salt and pepper and serve.

· 4 × 160g fillets of bass, scaled and pin boned

Cherry tomato sauce:
· 1 red onion, finely chopped
· 4 cloves garlic, minced
· 1 bay leaf and sprig of thyme
· 1 tbsp. tomato purée
· 1 glass white wine
· 100g cherry tomatoes, halved
· 60g basil, shredded
· 1 tsp. icing sugar
· 100ml olive oil
· 100ml stock (chicken works best)

Alternative fish: bream, mackerel, brill or mullet
Preparation time: 25 mins
Cooking time: 10 mins

(See page 27 for techniques)

PAN FRIED FILLETS OF BASS WITH CRISPY POLENTA AND CHERRY TOMATO SAUCE

1. Pre-heat oven to 240°C. **2.** Place a saucepan over a medium heat, add red onion and drizzle of olive oil. Season with sea salt and black pepper. Cook out low and slow for 5–8 minutes, then add garlic, thyme and bay leaf. **3.** Add tomato purée, cook out for 2 minutes, then add wine. Cook for a further 3–5 minutes, add stock and bring to a simmer then set aside. **4.** Place a roasting tray into a pre-heated oven. In a mixing bowl add cherry tomatoes, icing sugar, 50ml olive oil, sea salt and black pepper. Toss and pour cherry tomatoes and contents of the bowl into a hot roasting tray and bake. Every few minutes remove tray from oven and carefully pour off excess liquid into your pot containing onions and tomato purée. Pouring off the liquid and replacing tomatoes back in a hot oven gives the sauce a beautiful roast flavour. **5.** Roast tomatoes for approximately 15 minutes until they start to colour then remove tray from the oven. Add 100ml of water to the roasting tray and 'de-glaze' as you would if you were making a roast gravy – pour all the tray's contents into the pot containing onions and tomato purée. Return to the heat. Add basil and 50ml of olive oil, taste and adjust seasoning. Set aside. **6.** Place 2 frying pans over a high heat, season bass fillets with sea salt and black pepper. Place a drizzle of oil and a knob of butter into the pans, once butter starts to turn brown, carefully add bass fillets into pans skin side down. Shake pans to make sure fish doesn't stick. Cook until skin is golden, carefully turn fillets, turn off heat and rest fillets for 2 minutes and they're done. **7.** To finish, spoon warm cherry tomato sauce into plates and top with bass fillets. Serve with some green veg and polenta fries (see page 184).

Serves 4
· 4 × 160–180g pale smoked
  haddock fillets (no bones)
· 4 fresh as possible free range
  eggs
· vinegar
· white wine cream
  (see page 171)
· ½ tbsp. wholegrain mustard
· 1 tsp. chopped tarragon

Alternative fish: smoked whiting,
smoked cod or smoked mackerel
Preparation time: 20 mins
Cooking time: 10 mins

GRILLED PALE SMOKED HADDOCK WITH SOFT POACHED EGG

1. For the sauce, follow the instructions for white wine cream (see page 171) which can be made ahead of time. As you reheat the sauce, stir in wholegrain mustard and tarragon. **2.** Bring a deep pot 3 quarters filled with water to the boil, ready for poaching eggs. **3.** Pre-heat grill/oven to max. **4.** Fish should already be salted so just season with black pepper. Drizzle fillets with oil, slide under grill and cook for 6–8 minutes. **5.** While fish is cooking, add a splash of vinegar to your boiling water, crack in eggs and poach until soft. **6.** To finish, carefully transfer haddock fillets to warm oval plates, top with soft poached egg and drizzle with plenty of mustard velouté. This dish works great with boiled new season potatoes and boiled or steamed seasonal vegetables.

Serves 4
- 8 mackerel fillets
- 6 'ripe' plum tomatoes
- 1 sprig rosemary, chopped
- 2 cloves garlic, minced
- 1 tsp. chilli flakes
- 30ml rapeseed oil
- 100g green beans

Salsa verde:
- 2 garlic cloves
- 1 tsp. Dijon mustard
- juice of ½ lemon (approx.)
- 50g capers, rinsed
- 2 anchovies
- 250ml rapeseed oil or extra virgin oil
- 80g basil
- 80g parsley

Alternative fish: bass, bream, mullet or herring
Preparation time: 30 mins
Cooking time: 10 mins

(See page 27 for techniques)

GRILLED MACKEREL WITH CHILLI ROAST TOMATOES, GREEN BEANS AND SALSA VERDE

1. Pre-heat your oven on the grill/oven setting to 250°C.
2. Season mackerel fillets with sea salt and black pepper, drizzle with rapeseed oil on a baking sheet and set aside.
3. Cut plum tomatoes in half, mix together with rosemary, chilli flakes, garlic and oil. Brush or toss tomatoes in chilli oil mix and place on a rack with a baking sheet underneath. Season with plenty of sea salt. Place into the bottom of your pre-heated oven for 20–30 minutes. Tomatoes can be made ahead of time and simply pre-heated before serving. **4.** Cook green beans in salted water. Once green beans enter the water this should take about the same amount of time to grill the mackerel, 5–7 minutes. **5.** Drizzle the plates with salsa verde, place the roast tomatoes in the centre, top with the green beans, then mackerel and serve.

SALSA VERDE
1. Process all the ingredients to a smooth paste, adjust consistency with oil and add more lemon juice to taste.

Serves 4
· 4 lemon sole (no fins,
  no head, skinned)
· 200g herb butter
· 160g fresh mussels (cleaned)
· 2 plum tomatoes,
  chopped (no seeds),
  season with sea salt
· 1 lemon, cut into wedges

Herb butter:
· 4 shallots, sliced
· 4 cloves garlic, minced
· 1 glass white wine
· 50g parsley
· 50g chervil
· 50g tarragon
· 450g butter, diced
  (fridge cold)
· juice of 1 lemon

Alternative fish: plaice, brill,
Dover or megrim
Preparation time: 20 mins
Cooking time: 15 mins

(See page 27 for techniques)

GRILLED LEMON SOLE WITH MUSSELS AND HERB BUTTER

1. Pre-heat oven to 250°C – use grill/oven setting.
2. Drizzle sole with a little rapeseed oil, season both sides with sea salt and black pepper. Place sole on a baking sheet. Pop into the top shelf of the oven, cook for 5 minutes, remove from oven and rest for 3–5 minutes. **3.** While fish is resting, place a large pot with a tight fitting lid over a high heat. Once pot is 'smoking' hot, add mussels and tomatoes. Replace lid and give the pot a good shake. **4.** Pop the sole back into the oven to bring back up to temperature. Cook the mussels until opened, carefully pour off 3 quarters mussel liquor, place back on the heat and add 200g of herb butter and cook for 2 minutes. **5.** To serve, place sole onto an oval plate and spoon over mussels and butter sauce.

HERB BUTTER

1. Over medium heat in a saucepan, fry shallots and garlic with sea salt and black pepper for 3 minutes but do not colour. **2.** Then add wine, reduce until almost evaporated. Remove from heat. Add a quarter of the butter, mix, then pour into a food processor and purée. **3.** Add the rest of the butter and process until smooth, then add the herbs and lemon juice. **4.** Lay out a sheet of cling film. Place a quarter of the butter in the middle and roll into a sausage shape. Repeat 3 times. **5.** Butter will keep refrigerated for a week. Freezes well and keeps for 2 months.

'Butter works well with all fish. Also great with new potatoes and pasta.'

Serves 4
- 12 large king scallops (roe removed)
- 200g fresh greens (rocket leaf, chard, baby spinach)
- 100g diced tomatoes (no seeds)
- 440g dried linguine ('de Cecco' brand)

Garlic chilli oil:
- 2 red onions, finely chopped
- 2 red chillies, finely chopped (seeds in)
- 4 anchovy fillets, minced
- 1 sprig of thyme
- 1 bay leaf
- 4 cloves of garlic, minced
- 100g sun blushed tomatoes in oil, process to pulp
- juice of 1 lemon
- ¼ lemon zested with veg peeler
- rapeseed oil or olive oil
- 80g basil, optional
- sea salt and black pepper

Alternative fish: prawn, monkfish, salt cod or crab
Preparation time: 20 mins
Cooking time: 10 mins

SEARED SCALLOPS WITH CHILLI GARLIC OIL AND WILTED GREENS

1. Bring a large pot of water up to a hard boil, season with plenty of sea salt, add pasta and cook for 10 minutes. Warm the chilli oil in a separate pot along with seasoned diced tomato. **2.** Cut scallops in half, place 'cut side' facing up on a baking sheet and season with sea salt and black pepper. **3.** Over a high heat, place 2 non-stick frying pans, add a little oil and butter. When the butter starts to turn brown, quickly and carefully place the scallops 'cut side' down into the frying pan. Cook until golden and turn scallops then remove from heat and keep in the pan – they're cooked! **4.** Add hot cooked pasta to warm garlic chilli oil, toss in greens and approximately 2 tablespoons of pasta cooking water. Mix together, split between 4 plates and top with scallops – sprinkle with gremolata (see page 178) and parmesan (optional).

GARLIC CHILLI OIL

1. Cook onions in a saucepan over medium to low heat, season with sea salt and black pepper. Add thyme and bay leaf and cook until onions are soft and have no colour. **2.** Then add chilli, garlic and anchovies, cook out for 3 minutes then add all other ingredients and remove from heat. Adjust consistency with rapeseed oil. Store in fridge for up to 1 week. Finish with chopped basil.

Serves 4
· 4 large fillets of seabream
  (skin on, scaled and pin boned)
· 250g orzo (rice shaped pasta)
· 1 punnet of cherry tomatoes,
  quartered
· 200g baby spinach
· 1 bunch scallions, finely
  chopped
· 1 bulb fennel, shaved
· 1 bunch basil, torn

Gremolata:
· ½ bunch parsley, finely chopped
· zest of 1 lemon
· 2 large cloves of garlic, minced
Mix all of the above together

Alternative fish: bass, salmon,
hake, cod
Preparation time: 15 mins
Cooking time: 20 mins

(See page 27 for techniques)

SEABREAM WITH WARM ORZO SALAD AND LEMON OIL

1. Cook orzo following the cooking instructions on the packet. Once cooked, strain and keep 100ml of pasta water for later. Toss the orzo in a little lemon oil (see page 180) and keep at room temperature. **2.** Season the seabream with sea salt and black pepper, brush lightly with oil and grill under a medium to hot grill for 5–8 minutes. **3.** Whilst fish is cooking, in a large flat bottom pan, heat tomatoes, 100ml of lemon oil, sea salt and black pepper over a high heat for 2 minutes. Then add scallions, for 1 minute, then add cooked orzo, spinach, fennel and basil. Adjust the seasoning and add a couple of tablespoons of pasta water. **4.** Spoon into 4 bowls, top with cooked seabream and sprinkle with gremolata.

Serves 4

· 4 × 160g hake fillets (no skin, no bone)

Marinade:
· 1 clove garlic, minced
· ½ tsp. ginger, minced
· ½ tsp. garam masala
· 1 tsp. Madras curry
· oil to moisten

Chickpea curry:
· 50ml oil
· 2 red onions, chopped
· 2 cloves garlic, minced
· 1 tsp. ginger, minced
· 1 black cardamom pod
· ¼ tsp. mustard seeds
  (lightly toasted and ground
  in pestle and mortar)
· 2 green cardamom pods
· 2cm piece of cassia black
· 1 tbsp. curry powder
· 1 bay leaf
· 2 tbsp. tomato purée
· 1 tsp. tamarind concentrate
· 1 tsp. grated jaggery or demerara
· 100g cooked chickpeas (tinned),
  rinsed and drained
· 100g cooked baby potatoes
· 4 plum tomatoes, chopped
  (no seeds)
· 200g spinach leaves (washed)
· 80g fresh coriander, chopped
· fish sauce for seasoning
· 100ml stock (fish or chicken)

Alternative fish: salmon, tuna,
swordfish or cod
Preparation time: 20 mins
Cooking time: 20 mins

(See page 27 for techniques)

SPICED FILLETS OF HAKE WITH SPINACH AND CHICKPEA CURRY

MARINADE

1. For marinade, mix all ingredients and rub over hake fillets. Refrigerate for 1 hour or overnight.

1. In a large pot over a medium/low heat, add onions, sea salt and black pepper and cook until soft but do not colour (15 minutes). Then add garlic, ginger and all spices and aromates, cook for 2 minutes then add tamarind, sugar and tomato purée, cook out for 2 minutes. Then add stock and simmer over low heat, 5–10 minutes. **2.** To finish curry, add tomatoes, chickpeas, potatoes and bring back to a simmer. Add spinach, sea salt and black pepper, coriander and a little fish sauce to taste. **3.** Pre-heat oven to max.
4. Over a high heat, place 1 large or 2 smaller non-stick frying pans. Season hake on both sides with sea salt and black pepper. Put a drizzle of oil and a knob of butter into the pan. Once butter starts to turn brown, quickly add in hake. Shake pan to stop fish from sticking. Colour until golden, turn fish and slide pan into oven, 3–4 minutes. Remove from oven and rest in pan. **5.** To serve, spoon curry onto plates and top with hake.

'Seems like a lot of ingredients in this curry, but it is worth it. All the Asian ingredients are easy to find in any Asian supermarket and can be bought in small amounts.'

· 4 × 180g cod fillets (skin on
  and scaled)
· oil for cooking

Mushroom ragout:
· 4 cloves garlic, minced
· 2 shallots, small dice
· 100g button mushrooms,
  quartered
· 100g mixed wild mushrooms
  or cultivated, quarter half
  or slice the mushrooms
  depending on the size
  ('Oyster and shitake
  mushrooms are easy to get a
  hold of. My favourite are fresh
  girolles, harder to find, but
  totally worth the hassle.')
· 1 tbsp. dried porcini
· 1 glass white wine
· 200ml whipping cream
· 1 tbsp. chopped flat parsley
· 1 bay leaf and sprig of thyme

Alternative fish: hake, monkfish,
salmon or haddock
Preparation time: 40 mins
Cooking time: 15 mins

(See page 27 for techniques)

ROAST FILLET OF COD WITH MUSHROOM RAGOUT AND POTATO HERB GNOCCHI

1. To make the ragout, soak the dried porcini mushrooms in 50ml of water for 10 minutes, remove mushrooms, squeeze and chop fine. Set aside. **2.** In a large frying pan over a high heat, add a drizzle of oil, then shallots, mushrooms, sea salt and black pepper. Fry until golden (3–6 minutes) then add thyme, bay, chopped porcini and garlic, cook out for 2 minutes then add wine, cook until almost evaporated then add cream, taste for seasoning and finish with parsley. **3.** Sauce can be made ahead of time and reheated when ready. When reheating, don't let the sauce boil too much, thin sauce with water if it seems too thick and too rich.

HERB GNOCCHI
1. Make gnocchi (see page 186) ahead of time and refrigerate. **2.** Pan fry gnocchi when cooking cod, it should have around the same amount of time. **3.** Cook in a large non-stick pan with a drizzle of oil and a little butter. Let the butter turn golden brown before adding gnocchi, cook on both sides until golden over a medium heat.

COD
1. Pre-heat oven to max. **2.** Over high heat place 1 large or 2 regular non-stick frying pans. Add a drizzle of oil and a knob of butter, season cod on both sides with sea salt and pepper. Once butter starts to turn brown, quickly add the cod skin side down, give the pan a shake to prevent the fish from sticking. **3.** Continue to cook over a high heat until skin of the cod is golden, carefully turn fish and slide into hot oven for 2 minutes and the fish will be done.
4. To serve, arrange your gnocchi around a warm bowl, spoon mushroom ragout in the centre and top with cod.

DESSERTS

Serves 4

Crust:
· 250g digestive biscuits, crumbed
· 100g unsalted butter, melted
· ½ tsp. vanilla extract

Filling:
· 2 vanilla pods, split
· 125ml whipping cream
· 600g cream cheese
· 100g sugar
· pinch of salt
· 4 large eggs

Mixed berry compote:
· 1 punnet blackberries
· 1 punnet strawberries
· 1 punnet blueberries
· 2 tbsp. icing sugar

Preparation time: 15 mins
Cooking time: 1 hour

VANILLA CHEESECAKE WITH SEASONAL BERRIES

CRUST

1. Wrap outside of a 9 inch diameter springform pan.
2. Blend biscuits, butter, vanilla extract in a food processor until crumbs stick together. **3.** Press crumbs on bottom and halfway up the sides of prepared pan.

FILLING

1. Pre-heat oven to 175°C. Scrape seeds from vanilla pod into saucepan. **2.** Add cream and bring to a simmer, set aside and cool to room temperature, discard pods.
3. Blend cheese, sugar and salt in processor until very smooth, stopping and scraping down sides of the bowl.
4. Add cream and eggs, process for 5 seconds. **5.** Transfer filling to crust. **6.** Bake cake until sides puff slightly and centre is just set, about 50 minutes. **7.** Place uncovered hot cheesecake directly into fridge and chill for 6 hours or overnight.

MIXED BERRY COMPOTE

1. Take a quarter of the berries, add icing sugar and process until smooth. **2.** Pass berry pulp through a sieve. **3.** Mix your berry sauce with the rest of your berries and serve.

Serves 4

Cakes:

· 50g unsalted butter
· 350g dark chocolate
· 150g caster sugar
· 4 large eggs
· 1 tsp. vanilla extract
· 50g flour

Lemon scented strawberries:

· ½ lemon zest, cut into
  fine strips
· 50g sugar
· 50ml water
· 250g strawberries
· 1 tsp. vanilla extract

Preparation time: 15 mins
Cooking time: 15 mins

CHOCOLATE CAKE WITH CRÈME FRAICHE AND LEMON SCENTED STRAWBERRIES

1. Pre-heat oven 200°C. **2.** Lightly butter pudding moulds then dust with flour and cocoa powder. **3.** Place chocolate in a bowl and melt either in a microwave on a low setting or over pan of boiling water. **4.** In a bowl mixer using the whisk attachment, cream together the butter and sugar, gradually beat in the eggs and then add vanilla. **5.** Add the flour and then the chocolate. **6.** Whip until a smooth batter. **7.** Divide batter between moulds and bake for 10 minutes. **8.** Serve warm with crème fraiche and lemon scented strawberries.

LEMON SCENTED STRAWBERRIES

1. With a veg peeler, peel the zest off the lemon and cut into fine strips. **2.** Put lemon in a small pan and cover with cold water, bring to the boil. Strain. **3.** Put lemon strips back into the pan again, add sugar and water. **4.** Bring to a simmer, cook for 5 minutes – leave to cool. **5.** Add vanilla. Cut strawberries into quarters and add to lemon syrup and serve.

Serves 6
Topping:
· 300g pitted dates
· 300ml water
· 350g plain flour
· 3 tsp. baking powder
· 1½ tsp. baking soda
· 250g dark brown sugar
· 100g unsalted butter
  (room temperature)
· 3 large eggs

Toffee sauce:
· 175g unsalted butter
· 150g light brown sugar
· 125ml cream
· ½ tsp. vanilla extract

Preparation time: 15 mins
Cooking time: 40 mins

STICKY TOFFEE PUDDING

1. Pre-heat oven to 180°C. **2.** Butter a 13×9×2 inch metal baking pan, line bottom with greaseproof paper and butter greaseproof paper. **3.** Combine dates and water in a saucepan, bring to the boil, reduce heat and simmer until dates are tender and nearly all the water has evaporated (approximately 10 minutes). **4.** Transfer to processor and purée. **5.** Sift flour, baking powder and baking soda into a bowl. **6.** In a mixer, using the whisk attachment, cream together the butter and sugar. **7.** Add 1 egg at a time, beating well after each addition. **8.** Add flour mix in 3 batches, beat until smooth and mix in date purée. **9.** Spread batter in a prepared pan, bake until pudding is firm to touch, approximately 35 minutes. **10.** Cool in a pan on a rack.

TOFFEE SAUCE

1. Over a moderate heat in a saucepan, melt butter, then add brown sugar, bring mixture to the boil for 3 minutes. **2.** Stir in cream and vanilla, simmer sauce until it thickens slightly for about 5 minutes.

TO SERVE

Cut sticky toffee pudding into squares. Warm in the oven or microwave, cover with warm toffee sauce and serve with whipped cream or ice cream.

Serves 4–6
Topping:
· zest of ½ lemon
· 100g oats
· 75g granulated sugar
· 75g soft brown sugar
· 80g butter, diced and chilled
· 100g plain flour

Filling:
· 8 Granny Smith apples
· 50g butter
· 1 tsp. five spice powder
· ½ tsp. vanilla extract

Preparation time: 15 mins
Cooking time: 20 mins

SPICED APPLE AND OATMEAL CRUMBLE

TOPPING

1. Use a food processor to pulse all ingredients together until they form large crumbs.

FILLING

1. Peel and core the apples, chop into small pieces and place in a saucepan with sugar, butter, vanilla and spice. Cook over a low heat for 10 minutes until soft. **2.** Pre-heat oven to 225°C, fill a deep pie dish with filling and sprinkle over topping, bake for 15–20 minutes until top is golden and fruit starts to bubble at the sides. **3.** Serve with loads of ice cream and custard.

Serves 6
· 1 vanilla pod, split in half
· 200ml cream
· 225ml buttermilk
· ½ tin condensed milk
· 2 gelatine leaves, soaked
  in cold water

Plum compote:
· 200g ripe plums, stoned
  and quartered
· 1 tbsp. plum brandy or port
· 50g unsalted butter
· 100g caster sugar

Preparation time: 10 mins
Cooking time: 2 mins

BUTTERMILK PANNA COTTA WITH PLUM COMPOTE

1. In a saucepan, add cream, scrape vanilla seeds from pod, add both seeds and pod to cream, bring to the boil and remove. **2.** Remove gelatine from the cold water, gently squeeze it and add it to the hot cream and vanilla. **3.** Strain into a clean bowl, add condensed milk and buttermilk, mix well and pour into moulds. **4.** Refrigerate for 6 hours or overnight.

PLUM COMPOTE

1. Toss plums and sugar together. **2.** Place non-stick frying pan over a high heat and add butter. When butter just starts to turn brown, carefully add plums and sugar, reduce heat and cook out for 5–10 minutes. **3.** Add brandy/port and cook until plums soften. Serve at room temperature.

'Both panna cotta and plum compote are best made the day before, serve with shortbread or a cookie.'

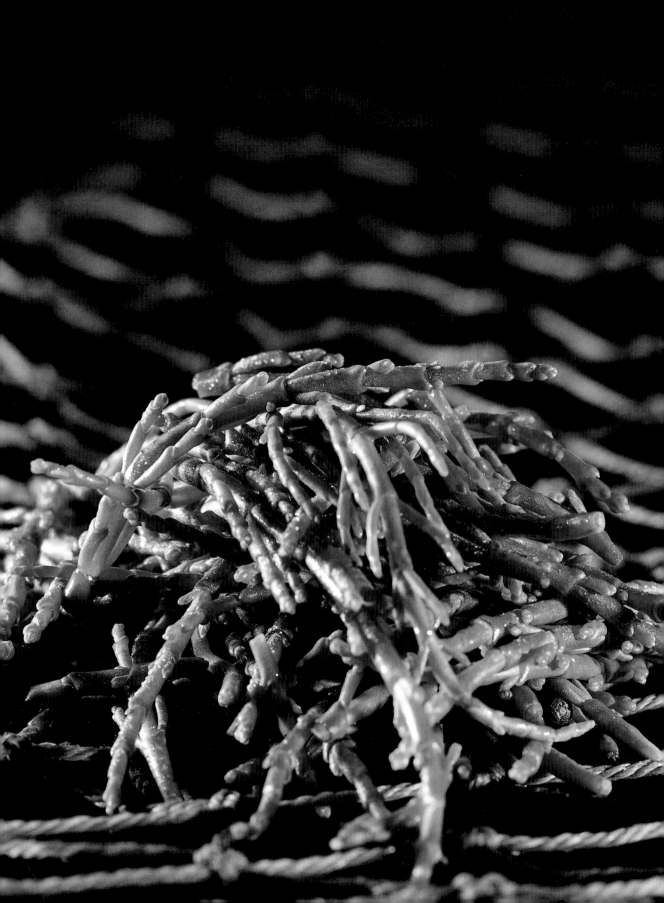

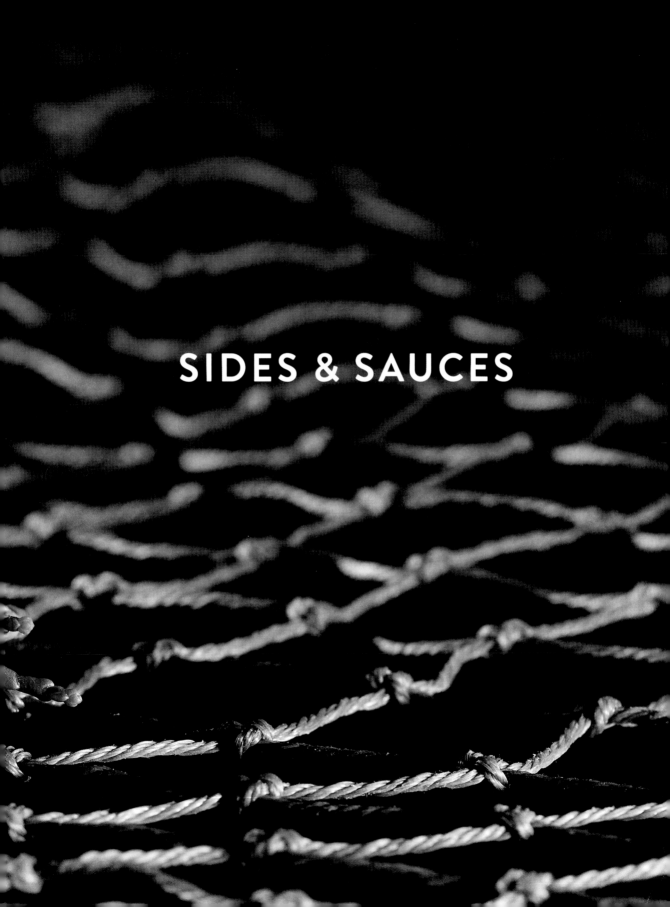

SIDES & SAUCES

SHELLFISH STOCK

Makes 3l
· 1kg shells
  (lobster, salmon, crab)
· 150ml white wine
· 1 onion
· 1 carrot
· 1 celery stalk
· 1 leek
· 4 tbsp. tomato paste
· 1 sprig thyme
· 1 bay leaf
· 1 bulb garlic
· 1 star anise
· 8 strands saffron

Preparation time: 10 mins
Cooking time: 1hr 15 mins

1. In a large roasting tray, roast shells in a hot oven for 10 minutes. 2. While shells roast, roughly chop veg, place in a large pot, add a drizzle of oil and sauté until golden brown. 3. Then add wine, cook until wine has totally evaporated, then add tomato paste and cook out for 3 minutes. 4. To the pot add shells, all other ingredients and 4 litres of water, bring to the boil and simmer for an hour. 5. Remove pot and carefully strain through a fine sieve. 6. Cool and refrigerate until needed. Keeps refrigerated for 3 days. 7. Or place stock into a clean pot and over a high heat reduce to a quarter of the volume, cool and freeze, keeps frozen for 2 months.

'Roasting the shells greatly enhances the flavour.'

FISH STOCK

Makes 1.25l
· 500g white fish bones
  (no eyes, skin, gills or fins)
· ½ onion
· ½ carrot
· ½ fennel bulb
· 2 celery stocks
· 1 sprig thyme
· 100g herbs
  (parsley, chervil, dill, tarragon)
· 2 bay leaves
· 3 litres water

Preparation time: 10 mins
Cooking time: 20 mins

1. Chop all vegetables small, place in a large saucepan with fish bones and aromates. 2. Add water, bring to a simmer, cook for 20 minutes. 3. Strain into clean saucepan and return to the boil then reduce by half. 4. Strain into a bowl. 5. If not using immediately, freeze in small amounts for later use.

PESTO

Serves 4
· 200g basil
· 100g flat parsley
· 100g parmesan cheese
· 50g pine nuts, toasted
· 4 cloves garlic, minced
· 200ml olive oil

Preparation time: 5 mins

1. Put all of the ingredients in a blender or food processor and blend to a chunky paste.

SALSA VERDE

Serves 4
· 2 cloves garlic
· 1 tsp. Dijon mustard
· juice of ½ lemon (approx.)
· 50g capers, rinsed
· 2 anchovies
· 250ml rapeseed oil or extra virgin oil
· 80g basil
· 80g parsley

Preparation time: 10 mins

1. Put all of the ingredients in a blender or food processor and blend to a smooth paste, adjust consistency with oil and add more lemon juice to taste.

SAUCE VIERGE

Serves 4
· 2 cloves garlic, minced
· 50g shallots, finely chopped
· 100g ripe tomatoes, diced (no seeds)
· 150ml extra virgin olive oil
· juice of ½ lemon
· 1 tbsp. chopped tarragon
· 6 coriander seeds, toasted and crushed

Preparation time: 10 mins
Cooking time: 10 mins

1. Put the shallots, coriander seeds, tomatoes, garlic and olive oil in a saucepan, season with sea salt and pepper and gently heat for 3 minutes. Add lemon juice and herbs just before serving.

Serves 4

- 2 tbsp. chopped black pitted olives (Niçoise)
- 4 ripe plum tomatoes, diced small (no seeds)
- 2 shallots, minced
- 2 cloves garlic, minced
- 1 glass white wine
- 1 lemon, juiced
- 100ml lemon oil (see page 180)
- 1 tbsp. shredded basil
- 1 tbsp. chopped tarragon

Preparation time: 10 mins
Cooking time: 15 mins

ANTIBOISE SAUCE

1. In a small saucepan over a medium heat, cook shallots with a drizzle of oil, season. **2.** Add garlic, white wine and cook until almost evaporated. **3.** Then add tomatoes, season well with sea salt and black pepper, add olives, herbs and lemon oil, gently cook until tomatoes just start to turn soft. **4.** Add lemon juice and serve.

Serves 4

- 1 knob grated ginger
- 1 small white onion
- 2 cloves garlic, minced
- 2 tbsp. curry powder
- 1 tsp. turmeric
- 1 tsp. garam masala
- 1 tin coconut milk
- 250ml cream
- oil for cooking

Preparation time: 10 mins
Cooking time: 20 mins

KORMA SAUCE

1. In a food processor, process onion, ginger and garlic, then add curry, turmeric and garam marsala to form a paste.
2. Fry paste in a little oil then add coconut milk and cream. Bring to the boil.

HORSERADISH CREAM

Serves 4
· 2 tbsp. finely grated fresh
  horseradish
· 125g sour cream
· 1 tsp. lemon juice

Preparation time: 5 mins

1. Combine all of the ingredients, season with sea salt and black pepper.

CHAMPAGNE VINAIGRETTE

Serves 4
· 30ml champagne vinegar
· 100ml rapeseed oil
  or olive oil
· 1 clove garlic, minced
· 1 shallot, minced
· 1 tbsp. honey

Preparation time: 5 mins

1. Combine all of the ingredients, season with sea salt and black pepper.

TZATZIKI

Serves 4
· 1 cucumber (peeled, deseeded
  and grated)
· 2 cloves garlic, minced
· 1 tsp. lemon juice
· 400ml Greek yogurt
· 60g fresh mint, chopped

Preparation time: 20 mins

1. Season cucumber with salt, place in a sieve and allow to drain for 15 minutes. **2.** Squeeze dry and combine with all other ingredients.

Serves 4
· 1 small white onion,
  roughly chopped
· 4 cloves garlic, crushed
· ½ fennel bulb, sliced
  (optional)
· 1 bay leaf
· 1 sprig thyme
· 1 glass white wine
· 100g fish bones
· 400ml water
· 500ml cream

Variation
Wholegrain mustard cream add:
· 1 tbsp. wholegrain mustard
· 1 tsp. chopped chives

Variation
Herb veloute add:
· 1 tsp. parsley
· 1 tsp. tarragon
· 1 tsp. dill
· 1 tsp. chervil

Preparation time: 5 mins
Cooking time: 20 mins

WHITE WINE CREAM

1. Over a medium heat in a saucepan, add a drizzle of oil, onion, fennel, bones, bay, thyme, garlic, sea salt and black pepper. **2.** Add wine and reduce until totally evaporated. **3.** Add water and reduce until almost fully evaporated. **4.** Add cream, bring to the boil then pass though a fine sieve, check seasoning and serve.

Makes 250ml
· 200ml milk
· 1 fresh bay leaf
· 1 sprig thyme
· 4 black peppercorns
· 1 shallot, sliced
· 1½ tbsp. butter
· 1 tbsp. plain flour
· 50ml cream

Preparation time: 5 mins
Cooking time: 15 mins

BÉCHAMEL SAUCE

1. Put milk, aromates and shallots in a small saucepan. Bring to the boil and then remove from heat. **2.** Melt butter in a small saucepan, add flour and cook, stirring for 1 minute over medium heat. **3.** Remove from the heat and gradually add the milk mixture, whisking to make a small, smooth sauce. **4.** Place back on the heat, add cream, bring to a simmer, cook out to thicken and pass through a fine sieve.

CITRUS RELISH

Serves 4
- 1 grapefruit
- 1 orange
- 1 lime
- 1 lemon
- 1 chilli finely diced
  (no seeds)
- 1 tbsp. chopped chives
- ¼ tsp. ground cumin

Preparation time: 20 mins

1. For the salsa, segment all the citrus fruit. **2.** To do this with a sharp knife cut the top and bottom off the fruit. **3.** Carefully from the top to the bottom, remove the skin and pith, then cut in between the membrane, but not through the centre of the fruit. **4.** When all of the segments have been removed, squeeze the rest of the juice over segments. **5.** Mix segments with cumin, chilli and chives.

BLACK BEAN DRESSING

Serves 4
- 4 cloves garlic, minced
- ½ tsp. ginger, minced
- 2 tbsp. fermented Chinese black
  beans – rinsed, chopped and
  drained
- 50ml light soy sauce
- 2 tbsp. dry sherry
- 1 tbsp. lemon juice
- 1 tsp. caster sugar
- 4 tbsp. peanut oil
- 1 tbsp. coriander, chopped

Preparation time: 15 mins
Cooking time: 15 mins

1. Place saucepan over a medium to high heat. Add a drizzle of oil and fry ginger and garlic for 1 minute. **2.** As the garlic and ginger just starts to brown, add black beans and fry for 1 minute. **3.** Then add all other ingredients, except for the coriander, bring to a simmer, taste, adjust the balance of the lemon and the sugar if needed. **4.** Set aside to cool. **5.** Once cooled add the coriander. Keep dressing at room temperature until needed.

Serves 4
· 100ml clotted cream
· juice of ½ lemon
· zest of ½ lemon
· 2 tsp. wasabi powder
· 2 tbsp. chopped dill

Preparation time: 15 mins
Cooking time: 25 mins

WASABI CREAM

1. In a small bowl, mix wasabi and lemon juice. **2.** Then add dill and half of the cream. **3.** Mix well then gently mix in the remaining cream. **4.** Refrigerate for 20 minutes then serve.

Serves 4
· 1 tbsp. caster sugar
· 75g Dijon mustard
· ½ tbsp. red wine vinegar
· 175g rapeseed oil
  or olive oil
· 50g chopped dill

Preparation time: 10 mins

DILL SAUCE

1. Put all ingredients in a screw top jar and shake like crazy, then serve.

Serves 6–8
· 2 egg yolks
· 50ml lemon juice and
  ¼ tsp. zest
· 1 tsp. Dijon mustard
· 200ml light olive oil
· 1 bunch basil, leaves only

Preparation time: 15 mins

BASIL MAYO

1. Liquidise basil and oil together to make basil oil.
2. Then place egg yolk, lemon juice, zest, salt and pepper and Dijon in a food processor, start processor then slowly add oil in a steady stream until incorporated. **3.** If mayo is too thick, thin with a tablespoon of warm water. Keeps for 2–3 days refrigerated.

Serves 8
· 2 egg yolks
· 2 tsp. Dijon mustard
· 2 tbsp. white wine vinegar
· sea salt and pepper
· 300ml rapeseed oil

Preparation time: 5 mins

MAYO

1. Place yolks in a food processor and add salt, pepper, vinegar and mustard. Process and slowly add oil until mix starts to look like mayo. If mayo gets too thick, add a little water to thin it down. Once made, refrigerate. Keeps for 24 hours.

Serves 4
· 4 shallots, sliced
· 4 cloves garlic, minced
· 1 glass white wine
· 50g parsley
· 50g chervil
· 50g tarragon
· 450g butter, diced
  (fridge cold)
· juice of 1 lemon

Preparation time: 10 mins
Cooking time: 15 mins

HERB BUTTER

1. Over medium heat in a saucepan, fry shallots and garlic with sea salt and black pepper for 3 minutes but do not colour. **2.** Then add wine, reduce until almost evaporated. Remove from heat. Add a quarter of the butter, mix, then pour into a food processor and purée. **3.** Add the rest of the butter and process until smooth, then add the herbs and lemon juice. **4.** Lay out a sheet of cling film. Place a quarter of the butter in the middle and roll into a sausage shape. Repeat 3 times. **5.** Butter will keep refrigerated for a week. Freezes well and keeps for 2 months.

Serves 4
· 1 lemon, juiced
· 1 tbsp. honey
· 1 tsp. Dijon mustard
· 75ml rapeseed oil
· sea salt and pepper

Preparation time: 5 mins

HONEY MUSTARD DRESSING

1. Mix all of the ingredients together.

Serves 4
· 2 tbsp. white wine vinegar
· ½ tsp. sea salt
· 1 tsp. Dijon mustard
· 100ml rapeseed oil

Preparation time: 5 mins

STANDARD DRESSING

1. Mix all of the ingredients together.

SEAWEED BUTTER

Serves 6
· 250g salted butter, soft
· 50g nori seaweed
· 1 glass white wine
· 1 sprig thyme
· 2 tbsp. parsley, chopped
· 2 cloves garlic, minced
· 2 shallots, sliced
· juice of 1 lemon
· zest of ½ lemon

Preparation time: 10 mins
Cooking time: 15 mins

1. Over medium heat, in a small saucepan, add wine, seaweed, thyme, garlic and shallots, cook until liquid has almost evaporated. **2.** Transfer into a food processor and process until smooth. Leave to cool and add butter, parsley and the juice and zest of half a lemon. **3.** Process until smooth, taste and add salt or lemon if needed. **4.** Wrap finished butter in cling film. If refrigerated, will keep for a week (can also be frozen). **5.** Serve butter at room temperature.

SMOKED CHILLI BUTTER

Serves 4
· ½ bottle chipotle tabasco
· 150g soft butter
· ½ lemon zest, grated
· 1 tbsp. parsley, chopped
· pinch smoked paprika
· 4 cloves garlic, minced

Preparation time: 10 mins

1. Mix all of the ingredients together.

GREMOLATA

Serves 4
· zest of 1 lemon, grated
· 80g parsley
· 2 cloves garlic, minced

Variations: Add ½ red chilli to above for chilli gremolata

Preparation time: 5 mins

1. Mix all of the ingredients together.

ASIAN GREMOLATA

Serves 4
· zest of 2 limes
· 2 cloves garlic, minced
· 1 tsp. ginger, minced
· ½ chilli, minced
· 80g coriander, chopped

Preparation time: 5 mins

1. Mix all of the ingredients together.

Serves 4
- · 1 red onion
- · 4 cloves garlic, minced
- · 1 bay leaf and sprig of thyme
- · 1 tbsp. tomato purée
- · 1 glass white wine
- · 100g cherry tomatoes, halved
- · 60g basil, shredded
- · 1 tsp. icing sugar
- · 100ml olive oil
- · 100ml stock (chicken
  works best)

Preparation time: 15 mins
Cooking time: 30 mins

CHERRY TOMATO SAUCE

1. In a mixing bowl add cherry tomatoes, icing sugar, 50ml olive oil, sea salt and black pepper. **2.** Toss and pour cherry tomatoes and contents of the bowl into a hot roasting tray and bake. **3.** Every few minutes remove tray from oven and carefully pour off excess liquid into your pot containing onions and tomato purée. Pouring off the liquid and replacing tomatoes back in a hot oven gives the sauce a beautiful roast flavour. **4.** Roast tomatoes for approximately 15 minutes until they start to colour then remove tray from the oven. **5.** Add 100ml of water to the roasting tray and 'de-glaze' as you would if you were making a roast gravy – pour all the tray's contents into pot containing onions and tomato purée. **6.** Return to the heat. Add basil and 50ml of olive oil, taste and adjust seasoning.

Makes 100ml
· 1 sprig rosemary
· 1 sprig thyme
· 1 sprig oregano
· 2 cloves garlic
· 100ml olive oil

Preparation time: 10 mins

....

Makes 200ml
· 2 red onions, finely chopped
· 2 red chillies, finely chopped
  (seeds in)
· 4 anchovy fillets, minced
· 1 sprig of thyme
· 1 bay leaf
· 4 cloves of garlic, minced
· 100g sun blushed tomatoes
  in oil, process to pulp
· juice of 1 lemon
· ¼ lemon zested with
  veg peeler
· rapeseed oil or olive oil
· 80g basil, optional
· sea salt and black pepper

Preparation time: 15 mins

....

Makes 500ml
· 1 bay leaf
· 1 sprig thyme
· 1 lemon, zested with veg peeler
  and juiced
· 500ml rapeseed oil

Preparation time: 10 mins

HERB OIL

1. Process all ingredients until smooth. Keeps for 1 week.

....

CHILLI GARLIC OIL

1. Cook onions in a saucepan over medium to low heat, season with sea salt and black pepper. Add thyme and bay leaf and cook until onions are soft and have no colour.
2. Then add chilli, garlic and anchovies, cook for 3 minutes then add all other ingredients and remove from heat. Adjust consistency with rapeseed oil. Store in fridge for up to 1 week. Finish with chopped basil.

....

LEMON OIL

1. Place all ingredients into bowl, mix and cover with cling film. Remove lemon zest after 24 hours. Keeps for 1 week.

Serves 4
- · 9 strands of saffron
- · 4 shallots, chopped fine
- · 4 cloves garlic, minced
- · 1 sprig thyme
- · 1 bay leaf
- · 1 glass white wine
- · 1 lemon, juiced
- · 200ml stock (fish or chicken)
- · 50ml Broighter Gold
  Rapeseed Oil
- · 200g cherry tomatoes, halved
  and seasoned with sea salt
- · 80g basil, chopped

Preparation time: 15 mins
Cooking time: 20 mins

BROIGHTER GOLD VINAIGRETTE

1. In a medium saucepan over a low heat add shallots, garlic, thyme, bay leaf and sea salt and black pepper. **2.** Cook for 4 minutes (until soft), then add wine and saffron, turn up the heat and reduce until almost evaporated, then add stock. **3.** Reduce stock by 3 quarters (50ml). **4.** Remove from heat and add cherry tomatoes and rapeseed oil. Add lemon juice, basil and set aside.

Serves 4
- · 100g rocket
- · 100g fennel, shaved or
  sliced fine
- · sea salt and pepper
- · ½ lemon juiced
- · 1 tbsp. rapeseed oil

Preparation time: 10 mins

ROCKET AND FENNEL SALAD

1. Add shaved fennel to a bowl, season with sea salt and pepper, add rocket, lemon juice and oil. Serve immediately.

Serves 4
· 100g pickled white crab meat
· ¼ bunch scallions, chopped fine
· 50g grated carrot
· 150g white cabbage,
  shredded fine
· ½ cup mayo
· ¼ tsp. cayenne pepper
· 1 tbsp. ketchup

Preparation time: 15 mins

CRAB SLAW

1. In a large bowl add carrot, white cabbage, scallions, season with sea salt and cayenne pepper to taste, leave in the bowl for 20 minutes. **2.** Drain off any excess moisture, then add the rest of the ingredients and adjust seasoning. Keeps for up to 24 hours.

Serves 4
· 50g grated carrots
· 250g sliced Chinese leaf
  or baby gem
· 50g coriander
· 4 red radish, sliced
· 1 punnet mustard cress
· 4 scallions, sliced

Preparation time: 15 mins

NAPA SLAW

1. Mix all ingredients and dress with napa dressing (below) just before serving.

· *Serves 4*
· 2 tbsp. rice vinegar
· 3 tbsp. fish sauce
· 2 tbsp. lime juice
· 1 tbsp. grated palm sugar
  or brown sugar
· 1 red chilli, no seeds finely
  chopped

Preparation time: 15 mins

NAPA DRESSING

1. Mix all of the ingredients together.

POLENTA FRIES

Serves 4
· 100g polenta flour
  (coarse)
· 400ml of water
  (season with thyme,
  bay leaf, garlic and sea salt)
· 60g butter
· 60g mascarpone cheese
· 60g parmesan
· 1 beaten egg

Preparation time: 20 mins
Cooking time: 5 mins

1. Bring seasoned water to a rolling boil in a medium-sized saucepan. **2.** Pour in polenta flour, reduce heat to low and cook out for 10–15 minutes until polenta comes away from the sides of the pot as you stir, then add cheeses and butter, mix well, remove from heat and pour into a lightly greased baking sheet. **3.** Refrigerate for 1 hour then cut into chip shapes or squares. Flour polenta shapes, coat in egg wash, then roll in coarse polenta flour (can be made ahead of time). **4.** Shallow or deep fry until golden. **5.** Finish with gremolata.

TUSCAN FRIES

Serves 4
· 400g chips, either homemade
  or frozen
· 100g tapenade
· 100g parmesan
· 50g chopped parsley

Preparation time: 10 mins
Cooking time: 20 mins

1. Fry or oven bake fries until golden and crispy. **2.** Put the fries into a large bowl straight from the oven or fryer. **3.** Add parsley and tapenade, toss until fries are coated in tapenade, then serve and top with parmesan.

BÉARNAISE POTATOES

Serves 4
· 500g baby potatoes (new season
  Combers), cut into halves
· 75g minced shallots
· 50g chopped tarragon
· 50g chopped chervil
· 1 lemon, zest and juice
· 100g salted butter – local
  'Abernethy Butter' works best

Preparation time: 10 mins
Cooking time: 30 mins

1. Cook baby potatoes in salted water. **2.** Once potatoes are cooked strain and put back into a dry pan. Add all the other ingredients, cover with a lid and give them a good shake. **3.** Serve.

BASIC RISOTTO BASE

Serves 4
· 440g arborio rice
· 1,200ml stock,
  chicken or fish
· 1 glass white wine
· 1 onion, chopped
· 60g butter
· 50g parmesan, optional

Preparation time: 5 mins
Cooking time: 25 mins

1. Heat a large saucepan over medium heat, add half of the butter, onion, season with salt and cook out for 6–8 minutes until soft and golden. **2.** Add rice and cook for 2 minutes, then add wine, cook out until wine has been totally absorbed. **3.** Add a large ladle of hot stock, one at a time, stirring continuously until each ladle of stock is absorbed and the rice is al dente (around 15–20 minutes). **4.** At this stage you can remove from the heat and spread on a baking sheet and cool for later, or stir in remaining butter, parmesan and serve.

'The thought of cooking risotto tends to strike fear into even the most experienced cooks but like anything, the key is practice. The more you do it, the easier it gets. If your stock is seasoned and full of flavour, this will shine through the finished dish. Take your time and get it right and you will have an excellent foundation for a wide variety of risotto dishes tailored to your taste preferences.'

HERB GNOCCHI

Serves 4
· 250g washed potatoes
· 1 egg yolk
· 40g plain flour
· 40g potato flour
· 1 tbsp. chopped parsley
· 1 tbsp. chopped tarragon
· sea salt and black pepper

Preparation time: 40 mins
Cooking time: 10 mins

1. Over a high heat, bring a large pot of water to a rolling boil, season with plenty of salt. **2.** Combine all the ingredients together and roll into a large sausage, around 2cm width, then cut into 3cm long 'pillow-shaped' gnocchi. **3.** Drop gnocchi into boiling water, gnocchi will sink to the bottom, when they surface, cook for 1 minute, then strain. **4.** Serve immediately or cold and pan fried in butter to serve.

POTATO PANCAKES

Serves 4
· butter for cooking
· 500g fresh mashed potatoes
  (room temperature)
· 4 egg yolks
· 2 egg whites, lightly whisked
· 4 tbsp. of plain flour, sieved
· 1 tbsp. chopped dill
· 3 tbsp. cream
· lemon oil (see page 180)

Preparation time: 10 mins
Cooking time: 10 mins

1. Mix yolks, mash, dill and cream together in a large bowl. **2.** Add egg whites and flour, mix but don't overwork the pancake mix. Set aside. **3.** Bring a pot of water to the boil, add in whole eggs and set a timer for 7 minutes, remove and leave to rest for 2 minutes then peel. **4.** Place a large non-stick frying pan over a medium heat. Add a knob of butter. When butter just starts to turn brown, add a spoonful of pancake mix, mix should make 4 large pancakes in total. Shake pan so pancakes don't stick, then slide pan into oven for 2 minutes, remove pan and turn pancakes and slide back into the oven and bake for a further 3 minutes. Pancakes should be golden on both sides.

SMOKED SALMON GRATIN

Serves 4
· 500g potatoes, peeled and
  thinly sliced
· 100g smoked salmon
· 10g chives, finely chopped
· butter
· 300ml whipping cream
· 2 cloves garlic, minced
· pinch of grated nutmeg

1. Pre-heat oven to 180°C. **2.** Put garlic, cream and smoked salmon in a small saucepan and heat slowly, then add chives and nutmeg. **3.** Butter a gratin dish generously, then arrange the potato slices in layers, season each layer and ladle over some cream and smoked salmon mix. Cover with foil and bake for 45 minutes then remove foil and bake for further 30 minutes approximately (until top is golden brown). **4.** Insert knife into centre to check that all of the potatoes are cooked through. **5.** Remove from the oven.

'This dish is best served "family style" in the centre of the table.'

Serves 4
- 600g potatoes, peeled and cut in 2cm cubes
- ½ tsp. saffron
- bay leaf
- sprig of thyme
- 100g butter
- 50ml milk

Preparation time: 10 mins
Cooking time: 25 mins

SAFFRON MASH

1. Place cubed potatoes into large pot, add just enough water to cover the potatoes, sea salt, saffron, bay leaf and thyme. **2.** Bring to the boil and cover until potatoes are soft, remove thyme and bay leaf. **3.** Strain potatoes and mash. **4.** Put back onto the heat, add milk and butter, taste and adjust seasoning and consistency.

Serves 4
- 400g baby potatoes
- herb oil (see page 180)

Preparation time: 10 mins
Cooking time: 30 mins

HERB ROAST POTATOES

1. Pre-heat oven to 230°C. **2.** Cut potatoes in half and toss in a bowl with a drizzle of oil and plenty of salt and pepper. **3.** Place potatoes onto a roasting tray and pop into the oven. **4.** While potatoes are cooking, make the herb oil. **5.** After 20 mins, potatoes should be almost cooked. **6.** Remove from oven, drizzle over herb oil and place back into the oven for approximately 5–10 mins, then serve.

Serves 4
- 400g peeled potatoes, large Roosters or new season Maris Pipers
- 50g butter, soft
- 1 tbsp. Szechuan peppercorns
- 1 lime, zested
- 25g grated ginger
- 1 red chilli, minced (seeds in if you like it hot)
- 25g coriander, chopped fine
- 2 garlic cloves, minced

Preparation time: 10 mins
Cooking time: 25 mins

SZECHUAN FRIES

1. Pre-heat fryer to 140°C. **2.** Cut potatoes into chips. Blanch chips in fryer, until they are cooked through and still pale in colour. **3.** Remove and set aside (this can be done ahead of time). **4.** Combine all other ingredients. **5.** To finish, turn fryer up to 180°C, fry chips until golden, drain on kitchen roll, then in a large bowl, toss chips in Szechuan butter mix, coating all the chips. Season with sea salt and serve.

SAFFRON BAKED POTATOES

Serves 4
- · 500g baby potatoes, peeled and cut in 3cm thick circles
- · 1 bulb fennel, halved and sliced fine
- · 100g shallots, finely sliced
- · bay leaf
- · sprig of thyme
- · 2 cloves garlic, minced
- · fish bones
- · 20 saffron strands and 1 litre water (heat and infuse for 20 minutes)
- · 80g basil
- · 100g tomatoes, deseeded and roughly chopped

Preparation time: 10 mins
Cooking time: 45 mins

1. Pre-heat oven, medium-high. **2.** In a large stainless roasting dish over a medium heat, add drizzle of oil, shallots, fennel, salt and pepper, and then add garlic, bay, thyme, potatoes and fish bones. **3.** Season with lots of salt and pepper, then add saffron and water. **4.** Bring to the boil, adjust seasoning (liquid should taste slightly salty). **5.** Add butter, wrap with foil, bake in the oven for 30–40 minutes until potatoes are soft. **6.** Add tomatoes and basil just before serving.

FOCACCIA CRISPS

Serves 4
- · 1 focaccia
- · 50 ml rapeseed oil
- · 1 garlic clove

Preparation time: 5 mins
Cooking time: 10 mins

1. Pre-heat oven to 220°C. **2.** Cut focaccia into approximately 2mm slices, brush with oil, lay on a baking sheet and bake until golden, approximately 10 minutes. **3.** While focaccia crisps are still warm, gently rub each crisp with garlic clove. Crisps can be stored in an air tight container.

BROIGHTER GOLD RAPESEED OIL

Like all of the best inventions, Broighter Gold Rapeseed Oil was born of necessity, but its real heritage lies in a land steeped in history and a love of good food.

One evening, while making family dinner, farmer's wife Leona Kane ran out of cooking oil while her husband Richard was busy crushing oilseed for biodiesel.

Having always used olive oil for cooking, Leona decided to try some of her husband's filtered rapeseed oil.

The difference was immediate.

The smell was pleasant, the high cooking temperature of the oil meant the meat was perfectly cooked and the oil had a light, nutty flavour leaving food crispy – not oily.

It was liquid gold.

Which is certainly appropriate since the very land where Richard Kane now grows his rapeseed oil is known as the Golden Field because of the fabulous treasure trove that had lain undisturbed for centuries below its fertile soil.

It remained hidden until 1896 when an amazing Iron Age hoard, now housed in the National Museum of Ireland, consisting of a miniature golden boat, torc collar, necklace, bracelet and a bowl was unearthed by a local farmer.

That exquisite find provides the inspiration for the name of this oil.

In recent years, high-end, cold-pressed rapeseed oil has become all the rage.

Grown locally, its versatility and palpable health benefits have made it a stable ingredient and a favourite of chefs in restaurants throughout the country.

Rapeseed oil has half the saturated fat and ten times the amount of omega-3 than olive oil.

It also cooks to a higher temperature than olive oil – 220 degrees rather than 180 degrees – making it much more versatile to work with.

While it is excellent in cold dressings and marinades, the higher smoking point makes it perfect for stir-fries, roasting, and baking.

Having launched in 2008, Broighter Gold has already garnered a large number of awards and a devoted following of top chefs.

It was awarded the Ifex 2012 Overall Product of the Show, Best Product Packaging 2012, Great Taste Awards Gold 2012, and has been featured in The Bridgestone 2012 as well as in McKenna's Guide.

Since producing the very first bottle of Broighter Gold, direct from the Golden Field, the Kane's pride themselves on delivering the best of culinary excellence and have created a brand that is local and unique.

A great dish needs great ingredients and Broighter Gold Rapeseed Oil will give you a tasty and healthy foundation for even the most delicate recipes featured in this book.

BELFAST COOKERY SCHOOL

If this book has whetted your appetite to learn more about cooking great but simply prepared food then why not extend your skills with some hands-on tuition at the award-winning Belfast Cookery School?

Our cookery school was born out of a love for simple food prepared well and sharing a wealth of experience and skills with those keen to learn.

The school is open to all levels of experience and is designed to awaken, enliven or revitalise a passion for cooking with fresh ingredients and the best quality produce.

Under the expert guidance of our experienced chefs you will be given a step-by-step lesson in creating a delicious meal you can re-create time and again at home to impress family and friends.

The cookery school aims to be sustainably aware and source as much of the ingredients used from local food producers as possible and a range of local produce is available for purchase.

The Belfast school, located at Mourne Seafood Bar, is the first purpose-built cookery school in the city and offers the same high standards of tuition in a relaxed environment.

The city centre location makes it an ideal option if you want to get together with friends or colleagues for a fun but informative session culminating in a great meal you help prepare yourself - with the support of a top-class chef of course.

It doesn't get more rewarding than that! It's also a perfect option for the individual or couple who want to try an experience that is a little bit different.

And it's not all about seafood as the constantly changing menu of events and classes mean you can acquire new skills and tips across a wide variety of food ingredients and styles – from baking to barbequing!

There is a wide range of diverse courses available throughout the year to appeal to all ages and levels of ability offering a fun, relaxed learning experience.

The atmosphere in the school bubbles with the entertaining and interesting banter we are so famous for between friends, students and their chef teachers.

This makes a trip to Belfast Cookery School a dynamic and enjoyable learning experience and a great day or evening out.

Like the restaurants, the emphasis in the cookery school is on a relaxed and informal approach to preparing food and you will be encouraged to develop your skills to appeal to your own tastes. Please arrive hungry as during the course you will be preparing a meal for yourself washed down with two complimentary glasses of wine. The cookery school is also available for private bookings and lends itself to events such as birthdays and team building events.

Belfast Cookery school will empower you with the confidence to try new and exciting dishes while at the same time providing a memorable and highly enjoyable experience.

For more information on classes or to book go to:
www.belfastcookeryschool.com

INDEX

ACKNOWLEDGEMENTS

If any great chef is honest, they will tell you they got their passion for cooking from their mum. For mums, cooking is an act of love.

That's why I want to dedicate this book to my mum Margaret Rea whose apron strings I have always hung on to.

For the best mum, cook and friend…

I also want to pay tribute to our local fishermen who risk their lives daily to supply us with fresh fish and seafood from the ports of Kilkeel and Annalong.

I also want to acknowledge the fish farmers who battle with hostile winds and tides to bring us their bountiful harvests of oysters, mussels and salmon.

They are pioneers in one of Ireland's most promising new industries.

Of course all of this would not have been possible without the support, hard work and dedication of our staff, new and old, who have been with us every step of the way on this journey.

I want to express my deepest gratitude to them all – from the chefs who work so hard behind the scenes, to our front-of-house staff who are always ready with a smile and an answer to any question.

Last, but certainly not least, a heartfelt thank you to our fantastically loyal customers who have supported us from the first day we opened our doors.

'There are good ships, and there are wood ships, the ships that sail the sea. But the best ships are friendships, and may they always be.' – *Irish Proverb*